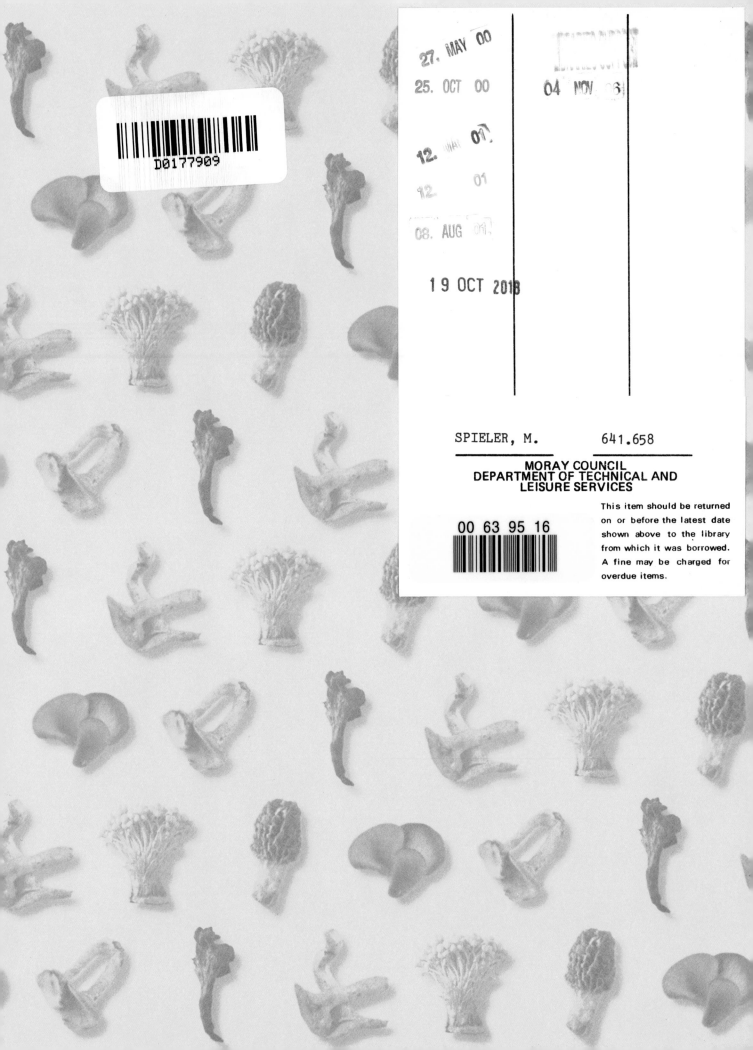

# a FEAST of MUSHROOMS

## Wild and Tamed

### MARLENA SPIELER

**APPLE**

A QUINTET BOOK

Published by The Apple Press
6 Blundell Street
London N7 9BH

ISBN 1-85076-857-9

This book was designed and produced by
Quintet Publishing Limited
6 Blundell Street
London N7 9BH

Creative Director: Richard Dewing
Art Director: Clare Reynolds
Designer: Steve West
Senior Editor: Sally Green
Editor: Rosie Hankin
Photographer: Philip Wilkins
Food Stylist: Jenny Stacey

Typeset in Great Britain by
Central Southern Typesetters, Eastbourne
Manufactured in Singapore by
Bright Arts Ptd Ltd.
Printed in Singapore by
Star Standard Industries (Pte.) Ltd.

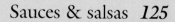

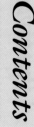

Contents

## Enoki

Enoki look like a cross between a long, tall white mushroom and a beansprout. They grow, in sterilized soil, in clumps. They are delicate and need no cooking. They are very tasty in sandwiches, as a garnish for sushi, and are also used in nouvelle cuisine, scattered over duck and kiwi salad, for example. Enoki are very good tossed at the last minute into soups and stir-fries, or in the filling of a pot sticker or spring roll. They are available fresh, usually vacuum packed.

You will find that enoki are usually sold in oriental and specialist food shops.

*To Prepare* Choose enoki that are white and firm, with no yellow discolouration or slimy edges. As they are grown in sterilized soil, they do not need to be cleaned, though the root cluster should be trimmed away. They are best raw in salads, or simmered in clear soup, or tossed into a stir-fry.

*Enoki grow in clumps, are delicate and don't need cooking.*

## Fairy Ring Champignon or Mushroom
### (Marasmius oreades)

These small mushrooms grow in circles on pastures or lawns. They are excellent for all sorts of dishes, especially in omelettes or pastas, or sautéed with chicken. In season—spring through winter—you may find them fresh, and they are available dried year round.

*To Prepare* To use fresh, brush off any dirt and trim the stalk ends. To use dry, rehydrate as you would any other mushroom.

**Field Mushrooms** See Champignon.

**Flat Black Mushroom, Flat Mushroom** See Cultivated, or Common, Mushrooms.

## Hedgehog Fungus

Also known as dentinums, hedgehog fungi have creamy white flesh that is best slowly cooked, when it tastes somewhat like chanterelles. Not often available in shops, you can occasionally find them fresh. They come in two sizes, one large, one smaller, and the cap varies from orange-brown to white, with a wide array of colours in between. They are very nice pan roasted with garlic and olive oil, or braised with meats or fish.

*To Prepare* Scrape off the spines on the underside of the cap; these give a bitter taste. Blanching tenderizes and takes off the bitter edge.

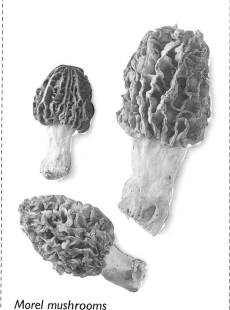

*Morel mushrooms*

## Honey Fungus

*Armillaria mellea* is sometimes called boot-lace fungus, because of its appearance, and is called famigliole in Italy, since it grows in 'little families' or clusters. It is edible when cooked, but is not eaten raw.

***To Prepare*** The fungus should be blanched for 5 minutes as it is mildly toxic. After blanching, sauté in garlicky butter or olive oil, and serve with pasta, or add to soups and stews. The stalks can be woody and tough, and should be discarded.

**Horn of Plenty** See Chanterelle

**Horse Mushroom** See Champignon

## Monkey's Head Fungus
### (also known as Lion's Mane)

This delicate white frilly specimen is very tasty indeed, though not easily found. It is sometimes sold under the name lion's head. When I first described a monkey's head fungus to someone, the only adjective that came to mind was 'fluffy', a fluffy white mushroom.

This coral or sponge-like fungus is particularly good in plain meat or vegetable stock, oriental-style, or as part of a gentle sauté of mixed mushrooms. I think it adds delicious interest and texture to stir-frys.

***To Prepare*** Soak in cold water several times for about 10 minutes each. This is because the many folds of the fungus are very attractive to tiny insects. Blanch the fungus for a minute, rinse in cold water, then add it at the last minute to your recipe.

## Morel Mushroom

Known in French as morilles, these ruffle-topped wild mushrooms are unsurpassed for flavour. I will never forget my first taste: slightly smoky, distinctly foresty, they tasted like nothing else I had ever eaten.

Morels come in many varieties, each one absolutely delicious. They range in colour from yellowish, through brown, through black. Sautéed, simmered, braised, or used in a sauce, they are superb to eat and to use to flavour other foods. Morels are one of those mushrooms, which, though both are wonderful, are almost better in their dried rather than fresh state, as the flavour is concentrated in the drying process.

***To Prepare*** Brush or wipe the fresh morels with damp absorbent kitchen paper, and trim the stalk ends. Then cut them in half and brush any soil from the inside. Morels should always be cooked, as they can disagree with some people when eaten raw.

# Bags of Mushrooms

*Crispy filo pastry parcels, the paper-thin dough twirled to form a fanlike top, contain several mouthfuls of delicious filling, giving a variety of tastes and textures.*

Serves 6–8

- 5 shallots, or ½ onion, chopped
- 3 garlic cloves, chopped
- 1–2 Tbsp olive oil or butter
- 225 g/8 oz mixed fresh mushrooms, thinly sliced
- 100 ml/4 fl oz dry white wine
- 100 ml/4 fl oz stock
- 2–3 Tbsp port
- 2 tsp cornflour
- 5 Tbsp cold water
- 4–5 heaped tablespoons crème fraîche
- sea salt and ground black pepper, to taste
- a grating of nutmeg
- 2 tsp fresh tarragon, roughly chopped
- 6 sheets filo pastry
- olive oil or melted butter, for brushing

**Preparation: 1 hour**

**Cooking time : 30-40 minutes**

❶ Preheat a 200°C/400°F/gas mark 6 oven. Sauté the shallots or onion with the garlic in the olive oil or butter until softened, then add the fresh mushrooms and sauté until lightly browned and tender.

❷ Pour in the wine and cook over high heat until the liquid is nearly evaporated. Add the stock and port, and cook over high heat until it also reduces to a thin sauce.

❸ Combine the cornflour with the water and stir it into the sauce, along with the crème fraîche, salt and pepper, nutmeg and tarragon. Simmer over medium-low heat for 5 minutes, or until thickened. Leave to cool, then taste for seasoning.

❹ To assemble the pastries, lay a sheet of filo pastry on a flat surface, brush with the olive oil or butter, then cover with a second sheet to form a double layer. Cut this into four equal squares.

❺ Into the centre of each square place a heaped tablespoon or two of the filling, then gather the four corners together in the centre, pressing tightly and neatly with your fingers to seal. Lift onto a baking sheet with a palette knife.

❻ Bake for 15–20 minutes until golden and crisp, then serve immediately.

The flavour of mushrooms is released by simmering in liquid. Just a few mushrooms can add great flavour to soup, and in the winter a handful of dried mushrooms can have a magical effect. Dried mushrooms, especially, are delicious with so many of the ingredients we enjoy in soup. They complement white beans, potatoes, barley and wild rice equally well.

And on its own, cooked only with well chosen seasoning, a soup of mushrooms can be a truly delightful experience.

*soups*

# Minestra alla Bosca

**Woodsey soup of turkey, wild rice and porcini** *This soup is good prepared with any sort of gamey meat, such as pheasant, or pork.*

SERVES 4–6

- 275 g/10 oz dark turkey meat, cut into bite-size pieces
- 1 onion, chopped
- ½ carrot, diced
- 1 bay leaf
- 3 Tbsp extra virgin olive oil
- 1 Tbsp flour
- 175 g/6 oz wild rice
- 2 potatoes, peeled and diced
- 1.2 litres/2 pints chicken, game or vegetable stock
- 25 g/1 oz dried mushrooms, such as porcini
- 225 g/8 oz common cultivated mushrooms, thinly sliced
- 4 Tbsp dry sherry, Madeira or Marsala
- salt and ground black pepper, to taste

**Preparation: 50 minutes**

**Cooking time : 1 hour**

❶ Sauté the turkey with the onion, carrot and bay leaf in 1 tablespoon of the olive oil until the onion is softened and the turkey lightly browned. Sprinkle in the flour and stir well to cook the flour through.

❷ Add the wild rice, potatoes and stock, and bring to the boil. Reduce the heat to a simmer and cook over low heat until the rice is nearly tender, about 45 minutes.

❸ Meanwhile, rehydrate the mushrooms by pouring 225 ml/ 8 fl oz hot, but not boiling, water over the mushrooms in a heatproof bowl. Cover and leave for about 30 minutes, then remove the mushrooms from the liquid and squeeze well over the bowl. Strain the soaking liquid and set aside.

❹ Sauté the sliced fresh mushrooms in the remaining olive oil, then add the rehydrated mushrooms, and cook together for a few minutes until the fresh mushrooms are lightly browned.

❺ Add the mushrooms to the soup mixture, along with the strained mushroom liquid. Pour in the sherry, Madeira, or Marsala, and season to taste. Serve immediately.

*Soups*

35

# Tranquility Broth of Many Mushrooms

SERVES 4–6

- 5 dried shiitake or Chinese black mushrooms
- 2 Tbsp dried Chinese black fungus (tree cloud or cloud ears)
- 750 ml/1¼ pints hot, but not boiling, water
- 1 onion, finely chopped
- 2 garlic cloves, chopped
- 750 ml/1¼ pints chicken or vegetable stock
- 5–7 thin slices of fresh root ginger
- 225 g/8 oz mixed fresh mushrooms, such as shiitake mushrooms, enoki, chanterelles, button, straw and curly white fungus
- 50 g/2 oz smoked tofu or smoked chicken breast, diced (optional)
- soy sauce, to taste

*This light and gentle mushroom broth gets its flavour from its wide assortment of mushrooms, both fresh and dried.*

**Preparation: 45 minutes**

**Cooking time : 20-30 minutes**

❶ Rehydrate the shiitake or Chinese black mushrooms and black fungus in the hot water. Leave to stand for 30 minutes, or until softened. Remove from the water and squeeze over the pan.

❷ Trim the hard pieces and stalk ends from the shiitake or Chinese black mushrooms and black fungus, and cut them into small strips. Strain the mushroom liquid. Return the trimmed and sliced shiitake or Chinese black mushrooms and black fungus to the strained liquid and set aside.

❸ Combine the onion, garlic, stock and ginger in a pan. Bring to the boil, reduce the heat and simmer gently for about 10 minutes.

❹ Add the mushroom liquid, rehydrated and fresh mushrooms to the soup. Simmer gently until the various mushrooms are cooked through, about 5–8 minutes.

❺ Add the diced, smoked tofu or chicken, if using, and season with soy sauce. Serve immediately.

# Monkey's Head Fungus, Chicken and Pea Soup

SERVES 4

- 1 monkey's head fungus, soaked and blanched (see page 15)
- 1 chicken breast, skinned and boned
- 1.2 litres/2 pints fresh chicken stock
- 3–4 Tbsp baby petits pois, fresh or frozen
- salt and ground black pepper, to taste
- a pinch of nutmeg
- grated Parmesan cheese

*The unusual quality of this frilly, fluffy mushroom demands a clear stock so that it may be seen and admired. Since the stock is such an important part of the dish, I recommend that you use a homemade or fresh, shop bought one rather than mix up a stock cube.*

*I added the strands of chicken for texture contrast, and the peas for the sheer beauty of their little dots of green.*

**Preparation: 5-10 minutes**

**Cooking time : 10 minutes**

❶ Cut the monkey's head fungus into bite-size pieces and the chicken breast into fine strips. Place the fungus, chicken strips and chicken stock in a saucepan. Bring to the boil, then add the peas, salt and pepper, and nutmeg. Bring to the boil again, to heat the peas through.

❷ Serve immediately, with Parmesan scattered over, if desired.

*soups*

# Potage aux Haricots et Porcini

**Creamy rustic purée of white beans and porcini** *Humble beans puréed with luxurious wild mushrooms create a classic soup throughout France's southwest. There is usually a scattering of shredded ham, such as prosciutto, and sometimes a shaving of truffle, a drizzle of truffle oil, or a scattering of diced creamy foie gras. Though the last ingredients aren't called for in the recipe, since the soup is lovely without them, if you happen to have any of them to hand, add them too, and feel decadent.*

SERVES 4–6

- 40 g/14 oz cooked white beans, such as cannellini
- 2.25 litres/4 pints stock, preferably ham
- 75 g/3 oz diced ham or bacon, such as pancetta or prosciutto
- 1 carrot, diced
- 1 baking potato, diced
- 2–3 tsp fresh thyme leaves
- 5 garlic cloves, roughly chopped
- 50 g/2 oz dried mushrooms such as porcini
- 225 ml/8 fl oz water
- 3 Tbsp brandy
- salt and ground black pepper, to taste
- 25 g/1 oz unsalted butter or 3 Tbsp double cream

........................................................

**Preparation: 15-20 minutes**

**Cooking time :**

**45 minutes-1hour**

........................................................

❶ In a saucepan, combine the beans with the stock, ham or bacon, carrot, potato, half the thyme and the garlic. Bring to the boil, then reduce the heat to low, and simmer until the vegetables are very tender and cooked through, about 30 minutes.

❷ Meanwhile, place the mushrooms with the water and brandy in a saucepan. Gradually bring to the boil, then reduce the heat and simmer until the mushrooms are tender, about 15 minutes.

❸ Remove the mushrooms from the liquid, chop roughly and add to the soup. Then strain the liquid, discarding the gritty pieces, and add the strained liquid to the soup.

❹ Whiz the soup in the blender or food processor until smooth. Taste for seasoning, then stir in the butter or cream. Serve immediately in warmed bowls, garnished with the reserved thyme.

# *Krupnik*

***Polish mushroom and barley soup with celeriac*** *A big bowl of steaming mushroom barley soup is great when it's really cold, during a blizzard in New York City or a winter in Poland both of which places are home to the following soup. I like to eat it with thick slices of seeded rye bread, spread with unsalted butter, and topped with a spring onion.*

*When, long ago, I ate it in Ratners, a dairy restaurant in New York's Lower East Side, and I asked about the soup, the owner took me aside and said: 'Here is my secret; always a celeriac'. He liked me!*

SERVES 4–6
- 1 carrot, sliced
- 1 onion, chopped
- 1 leek, chopped
- 25–40 g/1–1½ oz butter
- 250–350 g/9–12 oz barley
- 15 g/½ oz mixed dried mushrooms
- 1.5–1.8 litres/2½–3¼ pints stock
- 3 garlic cloves, cut into chunks (optional)
- ¼–½ celeriac, peeled and diced
- 2–3 bay leaves
- 1 large potato, diced
- salt and ground black pepper, to taste
- chopped fresh parsley, to serve

**Preparation: 15 minutes**
**Cooking time : 1 hour**

❶ Lightly sauté the carrot, onion and leek in the butter until softened, about 5–10 minutes. Add the barley, mushrooms, stock, garlic, if using, celeriac and bay leaves. Bring to the boil, reduce the heat and simmer until the barley is half tender, about 20 minutes.

❷ Add the potato and continue to cook until the potato and barley are very tender. If the soup is too thick, add more stock; if it is too thin, boil it down to reduce a little.

❸ Test for seasoning and serve with parsley scattered over.

TIP:
If you want a deeper flavour, use chicken or goose fat in place of the butter. For a healthier option, use vegetable oil.

Salads of mushrooms are delicious, varied, and extremely versatile. There are so many different types of mushrooms, and many of them can be eaten either raw or simply warmed through.

*salads*

# Salade Tiède aux Champignons,

## Chèvre et Asperges

**Warm salad of sautéed mushrooms, goat's cheese and asparagus** *This is quintessential bistro fare. You could, if you liked, add a handful of shredded prosciutto and/or toasted hazelnuts to this simply prepared but delicious salad.*

SERVES 4

- 350 g/12 oz small thin asparagus, tough ends broken off
- 3 shallots, chopped
- 2 garlic cloves, chopped
- 4 Tbsp olive oil
- 200 g/7 oz mixed salad greens
- salt and ground black pepper, to taste
- 1 Tbsp tarragon mustard
- 1 Tbsp raspberry or red wine vinegar
- 100 g/4 oz goat's cheese, crumbled or broken into small pieces
- 350 g/12 oz mixed fresh mushrooms, such as oyster, chanterelles, enoki, porcini and button, cut into strips or bite-size pieces
- 1 Tbsp balsamic vinegar or red wine
- 12 Tbsp chopped fresh chervil
- 2 Tbsp snipped fresh chives or chopped fresh tarragon

**Preparation: 15-20 minutes**
**Cooking time : 10 minutes**

❶ Cook the asparagus in rapidly boiling salted water until just tender and bright green, about 3 minutes. Drain, submerge in very cold water (add a few ice cubes to the water) to keep its bright green color and crisp texture, then drain once again. Set the asparagus aside while you prepare the rest of the salad.

❷ Mix 1 tablespoon of the chopped shallots with half the garlic and 1–2 tablespoon olive oil. Toss this with the greens, along with salt and pepper to taste.

❸ Mix 1 tablespoon olive oil with the tarragon mustard and the raspberry or red wine vinegar; stir well then pour over the greens and toss well. Arrange asparagus and goat's cheese over the top.

❹ Sauté the mushrooms over a medium-high heat, with the remaining shallots and garlic, in the remaining olive oil until lightly browned. Pour in the balsamic vinegar or red wine, season, and pour this hot mixture over the salad. Serve immediately, with the herbs scattered over.

*salads*

**45**

# Insalata di Ovoli e Tartuffi

**Salad of porcini, ovoli, enoki and truffles** *Sometimes I add fresh porcini to the ovoli, as both are sublime eaten raw. A handful of enoki, though not essential, is very appealing. Their long, graceful stalks look terribly foresty, adding to the intensely fungi theme of this salad.*

*The truffle topping can either be the white gems of Alba or the black nuggets of Norcia. If there is no fresh truffle, use truffle/porcini condiment or, as a last resort, drops of very fresh truffle oil.*

SERVES 4

- 6 ovoli mushrooms or porcini, or 3 of each
- 1 celery stick, cut into julienne strips
- 65 g/2½ oz enoki mushrooms, whole but separated
- 25–50 g/1–2 oz Parmesan cheese, cut into fine shavings
- juice of ½ lemon
- 4–6 Tbsp extra virgin olive oil
- 1 truffle, shredded, or several dollops of truffle/porcini condiment

**Preparation: 15-20 minutes**

❶ Slice the mushrooms very thinly, then toss with the celery, enoki and Parmesan. Dress with lemon juice and olive oil.

❷ Sprinkle the top with the truffle or add the condiment to the salad, and serve, offering extra olive oil and lemon at the table.

*salads*

*Ah, the thought of pasta and porcini. On my first visit to Florence, I was so obsessed with porcini that I soon gave up on gallery-going and planned my cultural forays by where the next dish of pasta al funghi was likely to be.*

*I have since found out that porcini is delicious not only on pasta, but in it as well. And it's not only porcini that is so terrific with pasta; nearly any type of mushroom is. Whether it is awash in a sauce of cream, tomatoes, butter or olive oil, there are few things more utterly enticing.*

*pasta*

# Pappardelle con Carciofi e Funghi

**Creamy artichoke and wild mushroom sauce over tagliatelle or lasagne sheets** *Artichokes pair so easily, so happily, so very deliciously with porcini. Both taste of a forest in the Mediterranean, and both are very good when tossed with pasta.*

SERVES 4

- 2 artichokes
- 50–75 g/2–3 oz mixed dried wild mushrooms or 350 g/12 oz fresh mushrooms
- 1 onion, chopped
- 4 garlic cloves, roughly chopped
- 40 g/1½ oz butter, plus a little extra for buttering the pasta
- 100 ml/4 fl oz hot water, if using dried mushrooms, or stock
- 225 ml/8 fl oz whipping cream
- 100 g/4 oz ricotta cheese or soured cream
- a few drops lemon juice
- salt and ground black pepper, to taste
- a few gratings of nutmeg
- 225 g/8 oz tagliatelle or egg lasagne sheets
- 225 g/8 oz cheese, such as Gruyère, Emmental, Parmesan, asiago or a combination, grated

**Preparation: 30 minutes**
**Cooking time : 15-20 minutes**

❶ Snap the outer leaves off of the artichokes by bending them back crisply. When you reach the tender inner leaves, stop, then trim the base of the artichoke using a paring knife. Slice off the sharp prickly tops that are left, then cut each artichoke heart into quarters and pare out the thistle-like centre.

❷ Blanch the artichoke hearts for about 3 minutes in boiling water to which you have added a squeeze of lemon. Remove, rinse in cold water and, when cool enough to handle, slice thickly.

❸ If using dried mushrooms, rehydrate them, then remove from the water, squeeze dry and cut into bite-size pieces. Reserve the mushroom liquid.

❹ Lightly sauté the onion and garlic in the butter until softened, then add the mushrooms and artichoke slices. Raise the heat and sauté, until the vegetables are lightly browned in spots.

❺ Pour in the mushroom liquid or stock, bring to the boil, then reduce over high heat. Pour in the whipping cream and cook a few minutes more.

❻ Lower the heat, stir in the ricotta cheese or soured cream, and the lemon juice, salt and pepper, and nutmeg. Set aside while you cook the pasta.

❼ Cook the pasta, according to the instructions on the packet, until just tender. Drain carefully so as not to break too much of the pasta, then lightly toss with a little butter, and arrange on a platter.

❽ Pour the artichoke and mushroom sauce over, then blanket with the grated cheese, and toss lightly. Serve immediately.

........................................
TIP:
Vary the mushrooms you use according to your personal taste and availability. Try porcini, chanterelles, morels and other fragrant varieties.

# Tagliatelle con Porcini e Mascarpone

**Flat thin noodles with porcini and mascarpone cheese** *Porcini, mascarpone cheese and fresh Parmesan are served on tender pasta, with thin shreds of salty prosciutto. This dish is delicious with either fresh or dried porcini.*

SERVES 4 AS AN APPETIZER, 2 AS A MAIN COURSE

- 350 g/12 oz fresh porcini, or 50 g/2 oz dried porcini, rehydrated in 100 ml/4 fl oz water, then squeezed dry
- 25 g/1 oz butter
- 2 garlic cloves, chopped
- 2 Tbsp dry white wine
- 50 g/2 oz prosciutto, thinly sliced
- 350 g/12 oz tagliatelle or fettucine, preferably fresh
- 3–5 heaped tablespoons mascarpone cheese
- freshly grated Parmesan cheese, to serve

**Preparation: 10 minutes**
**Cooking time : 10 minutes**

TIP:

If using dried porcini, strain the soaking liquid carefully, then boil rapidly to reduce by about half, and add to the cooked pasta.

❶ Sauté the mushrooms in the butter with the garlic until just tender, then add the wine and cook until it has nearly evaporated. Stir in the prosciutto and remove from the heat.

❷ Cook the pasta in rapidly boiling salted water, then drain and toss it with the mushrooms, mascarpone and Parmesan as desired. Serve in warmed shallow soup bowls, Italian-style, as they retain the heat and keep the pasta soft and supple.

# Penne con Funghi, Asparagi e Salsa Rossa

**Penne with mixed mushrooms, asparagus and tomato-cream sauce** *Sautéed mushrooms and asparagus pieces, simmered in a tomato-cream sauce, then tossed with quill-shaped penne and fresh basil, make a flavourful, rich Italian pasta.*

Serves 4

- 1 onion, roughly chopped
- 4 garlic cloves, roughly chopped
- 3 Tbsp olive oil or butter, plus a little extra to finish
- 350 g/12 oz mixed mushrooms, cut into bite-size pieces
- salt and ground black pepper, to taste
- 450 g/1 lb fresh tomatoes, finely chopped, or 225 g/8 oz canned chopped tomatoes in their juice
- ¼–½ tsp sugar
- 350 ml/12 fl oz double cream
- 25–50 g/1–2 oz fresh sweet basil, torn
- 350–450 g/12–16 oz penne
- 1 bunch thin asparagus, tough ends broken off, cut into bite-size lengths
- 4–6 Tbsp grated Parmesan cheese

**Preparation: 30 minutes**
**Cooking time : 15 minutes**

❶ Sauté the onion and garlic in the olive oil or butter, until softened. Then add the mushrooms and cook, stirring occasionally to prevent sticking. Season, then pour in the tomatoes and add the sugar. Bring to the boil and cook, stirring, a few minutes more. Then add the cream and about a third of the basil. Taste, adjust seasoning, and remove from the heat.

❷ Cook the pasta until half done, then add the asparagus and finish cooking. The pasta should be *al dente* and the vegetables just tender.

❸ Toss the hot pasta and asparagus with the tomato-mushroom sauce, then the Parmesan, remaining basil and a little oil or butter.

❹ Serve while piping hot on warmed plates.

# Tagliatelle con Fegatini

**Flat thin noodles with chicken liver, sausage and mushroom sauce** *Classically this is made without garlic, but I often add it anyhow since it is my passion. If you decide to include garlic, add about 3 cloves, roughly chopped, when you are sautéeing the prosciutto or bacon.*

*Not only can this sauce be served with pasta, it is wonderful spooned over a simple risotto.*

SERVES 4
- 1 onion, chopped
- 1 carrot, chopped
- 1 celery stick with leaves, chopped
- 2 Tbsp chopped fresh parsley
- 3–4 Tbsp olive oil
- 5 chicken livers, washed and diced
- 100 g/4 oz prosciutto or 4 slices of bacon, diced
- 1 Italian sausage, preferably fennel flavoured, cut into small pieces
- a handful of common cultivated mushrooms, quartered (optional)
- 25 g/1 oz dried mushrooms, preferably porcini, broken into small pieces
- 175 ml/6 fl oz stock
- 100 ml/4 fl oz dry red wine
- 675 g/1½ lb tomatoes, fresh or canned, diced
- 1 bay leaf
- a pinch of sugar
- salt and ground black pepper, to taste
- several leaves fresh sage, thyme and rosemary, chopped
- 450 g/1lb fresh thin, flat noodle-type pasta, such as tagliolini, fettucine or tagliatelle
- freshly grated Parmesan cheese, to serve

**Preparation: 15-20 minutes**
**Cooking time : 30-40 minutes**

❶ Lightly sauté the onion, carrot, celery and parsley in 3 tablespoons olive oil, then add the livers and a little more olive oil if you need it. Lightly brown the livers, stirring constantly.

❷ Add the proscuitto or bacon, the sausage and the fresh mushrooms, if using. Cook a few moments, then add the dried mushrooms, stock and wine. Cook over high heat for 5–10 minutes.

❸ Add the tomatoes, bay leaf and sugar. Bring to the boil, then reduce the heat and simmer over very low heat until the mixture thickens. Season with salt and pepper, as desired, and stir in the sage, thyme and rosemary.

❹ Cook the pasta until *al dente*, then drain and serve immediately with the sauce and a generous sprinkling of grated Parmesan cheese.

*pasta*

# Roasted Mushroom-topped Pasta Gratin

*When you eat the dish, you have a wonderful duet of the grated mushrooms melded into the pasta below and the accumulated juices of the mushrooms on top.*

Serves 4

- 450 g/1 lb small elbow macaroni
- 450 g/1 lb common cultivated, open-cap mushrooms
- 225 ml/8 fl oz crème fraîche
- 225 g/8 oz ricotta cheese
- 2 shallots, chopped
- 2–3 tsp chopped fresh tarragon
- 75–100 g/3–4 oz Parmesan cheese, freshly grated
- 5 garlic cloves, chopped
- 175–225 g/6–8 oz mature Cheddar or fontina cheese, grated
- 40–50 g/1½–2 oz butter
- salt and ground black pepper, to taste

---

**Preparation: 20 minutes**

**Cooking time : 30 minutes**

---

❶ Preheat a 200°C/400°F/gas mark 6 oven. Boil the macaroni until just *al dente* but still quite chewy. Drain and set aside.

❷ Shred the mushrooms, then toss half of them with the cooked pasta. Add the crème fraîche, ricotta cheese, shallots, half the tarragon, the Parmesan, half the garlic and the grated Cheddar or fontina.

❸ Turn this mixture out into a round or square shallow baking pan. Remove the stalks from the remaining mushrooms. Shred these and add them to the pasta, then shred the rest and spread over the top. Dot the mushrooms with the butter, then sprinkle with the remaining garlic, tarragon and salt and pepper.

❹ Bake for 20 minutes, or until the pasta is heated. Serve immediately.

# Macaronis aux Champignons

*et Petits Pois, en Gratin*

**Gratin of macaroni with wild mushrooms and peas** Mushrooms and pasta are natural partners and make wonderful gratins. Add any sort of bright vegetable for variety and interest. When artichokes or asparagus are in season, they go into my gratin instead of the peas.

SERVES 4

- 50 g/2 oz small elbow macaroni
- 225 g/8 oz baby peas, fresh or frozen
- salt, to taste
- 225–350 g/8–12 oz mixed fresh wild mushrooms, or a mixture of white mushrooms and rehydrated dried mushrooms, diced
- 3 shallots, chopped
- 3 garlic cloves, chopped
- 40 g/1½ oz butter
- 3 Tbsp snipped fresh chives
- ground black pepper, to taste
- 3–4 Tbsp double cream
- 4–6 Tbsp each grated fontina (or Gruyère, asiago or mild white Cheddar, and Parmesan

**Preparation: 10 minutes**

**Cooking time : 30 minutes**

❶ Preheat a 190°C/375°F/gas mark 5 oven. Cook the pasta in rapidly boiling salted water until it is about half tender, then remove from the heat and drain. Toss with the peas. The pasta should be just short of *al dente* and the peas still bright green and perhaps a little crunchy.

❷ Sauté the mushrooms, shallots and garlic in the butter until the mushrooms are lightly browned, then remove from the heat and add the chives. Then toss with the pasta and peas. Season to taste.

❸ Layer half the pasta mixture in the base of a gratin or casserole dish, then drizzle with half the cream and half the cheese. Top with remaining pasta mixture and the remaining cheese, pouring the other half of the cream over the top.

❹ Bake in the oven for 20 minutes, or until the pasta is heated through and the cheese melted. If the pasta seems dry, add a little more cream. Serve immediately.

*pasta*

# Spaetzel with Mixed Mushrooms from the Fields

*Dumplings and mushrooms have a natural affinity—you cannot but enjoy the combination, whatever kind of dumpling you make and whichever sort of mushroom you use.*

SERVES 4

- 225–350 g/8-12 oz unbleached flour
- 1 tsp salt
- 2 eggs
- 100 ml/4 fl oz milk
- several gratings of nutmeg
- 40–50 g/1½–2 oz butter
- 4–5 shallots or 1 onion, chopped
- 3 garlic cloves, chopped
- 225 g/8 oz mixed fresh mushrooms, such as field mushrooms, mousserons, porcini and chanterelles, diced, or a combination of ordinary brown/white cultivated mushrooms mixed with several tablespoons rehydrated dried exotic mushrooms
- salt and ground black pepper, to taste
- 1 Tbsp chopped fresh parsley, to serve
- 1 Tbsp snipped fresh chives, to serve

**Preparation: 30 minutes**
**Cooking time : 15 minutes**

❶ Sift together the flour and salt. In a separate bowl, combine the eggs with the milk and nutmeg. Stir the liquid into the flour until you have a thick sticky batter.

❷ Bring a large pan of salted water to the boil then, using a spaetzel-maker or a colander with large holes set over the boiling water, pour in the batter and, using a large spoon, force it through the holes. The batter will form squiggly shapes that fall into the water. In about 5 minutes, tiny dumplings will bob up to the surface. Cover the pan and boil for 5 minutes more, removing the lid if the pan threatens to boil over.

❸ Drain the dumplings carefully, then place in a bowl of cold water for 15–30 minutes to firm up. Don't be tempted to omit this step or they will disintegrate into a sticky mess. You can keep them in water for up to 2 hours.

❹ Melt the butter, then sauté the shallots or onion. Add the garlic and mushrooms, and cook a few minutes until lightly browned and tender. Season with salt and pepper.

❺ When you are ready to serve, drain the spaetzels and toss with the hot mushrooms. Heat through gently, adding a little extra butter if needed. Serve hot, with parsley and chives scattered over.

# Gnocchi Verde con Funghi

**Spinach-ricotta dumplings with mushroom sauce** *Spinach-ricotta dumplings are delicious with all sorts of earthy wild mushroom sauces: lashings of cream and/or tomatoes, Madeira and deep-flavoured meat stock are all good enrichments. However simply sautéed mushrooms, with just a whiff of cream, are splendidly uncomplicated, and show off the mushrooms to perfection.*

SERVES 4
- 450 g/1 lb fresh spinach or 225 g/8 oz frozen
- 225 g/8 oz ricotta cheese
- 2 eggs, lightly beaten
- 6–8 Tbsp freshly grated Parmesan cheese, plus a little extra
- 6–8 Tbsp flour, plus extra for rolling dumplings in
- salt and ground black or white pepper, to taste
- ⅛–¼ tsp freshly grated nutmeg
- ½ onion, chopped
- 40–50 g/1½–2 oz butter, olive oil or a combination
- 3 garlic cloves, chopped
- 225 g/8 oz fresh wild mushrooms, such as porcini, ovoli or mixed exotic mushrooms, sliced
- 2 Tbsp brandy or dry white wine
- 2 Tbsp crème fraîche or double cream
- 1 Tbsp chopped fresh Italian parsley

**Preparation: 30 minutes**
**Cooking time : 35-40 minutes**

❶ Cook the fresh spinach until just cooked through and bright green, then drain, squeeze dry and chop. If using frozen chopped spinach, just defrost, drain and squeeze well.

❷ Combine the spinach with the ricotta cheese, eggs, Parmesan cheese, flour, salt and pepper, and nutmeg. Chill for at least 2 hours. (The mixture should be firm enough to hold a ball shape when you form it with two spoons.)

❸ Preheat a 200°C/400°F/gas mark 6 oven. Using two spoons, form dumplings of the spinach mixture and roll each in flour. Poach the dumplings, in batches, in lightly boiling salted water. Cook the dumplings for 5–7 minutes, until they float, then take them out with a slotted spoon, and set aside in a gratin dish or baking dish.

❹ Sauté the onion in the butter and/or olive oil, then add the garlic and mushrooms, and cook until lightly browned. Add the brandy or wine and cook over high heat until evaporated. Stir in the crème fraîche, or cream, and parsley. Spoon the sauce over and around the dumplings. Sprinkle generously with grated Parmesan, then bake for 15 minutes, or until the cheese is melted and lightly browned, and the dumplings are heated through. Serve immediately, with parsley scattered over.

# Lasagne alla Porcini

**Baked lasagne with creamy porcini sauce and chervil** This dish actually tastes best with the strong, concentrated flavour of dried, rather than fresh, porcini, and the mushroom liquid can then be used in the sauce. While most recipes are deliciously adaptable to nearly any fungi, use only porcini in this one, for the finest fragrance and flavour.

SERVES 4–6
- 50–75 g/2–3 oz dried porcini
- 450 ml/¾ pint water
- 5–8 shallots, chopped
- 65 g/2½ oz butter
- 3 Tbsp brandy
- 350 ml/12 fl oz single cream
- salt, ground black pepper, and a few gratings of nutmeg, to taste
- 275 g/10 oz lasagne noodles, preferably fresh
- 175–225 g/6–8 oz freshly grated Parmesan cheese
- 3–5 Tbsp fresh chervil leaves, roughly chopped

**Preparation: 1 hour**

**Cooking time : 1 hour**

❶ Place the porcini and water in a saucepan and bring to the boil. Reduce the heat and simmer over medium heat for 5–10 minutes, or until the mushrooms have softened. Remove the mushrooms from the liquid, chop roughly and set aside. Strain the liquid for the sauce.

❷ Sauté the shallots in the butter until softened, then add the mushrooms and cook for a few moments. Add the brandy and cook over high heat until evaporated. It may flame, so avert your face.

❸ When the brandy has evaporated, ladle in 100 ml/4 fl oz of the mushroom liquid, then cook over high heat until nearly evaporated. Repeat until all the liquid is used up and you have a concentrated, thin reduction. Now add the cream and simmer for 5–10 minutes. Season with salt, pepper and nutmeg, and set aside.

❹ Preheat a 190°C/375°F/gas mark 5 oven. Cook the lasagne noodles in boiling salted water, a few at a time to keep them from sticking. (You can use fresh noodles without first cooking them, but I find that the result can be a little heavy.)

❺ As they are cooked, carefully take each noodle out and immediately place in cold water. This will make them easier to handle. Then place them in a very lightly oiled pan. Repeat until all of the noodles are cooked.

❻ In a 30 × 38 cm/12 × 15 inch buttered baking dish make a layer of lasagne noodles, letting the sheets hang over the sides to wrap over the layers of noodles as they are formed. Make a double layer, then ladle in about a quarter of the mushroom sauce, a quarter of the cheese and a sprinkling of the chervil. Repeat until mixture is used up, ending with the cheese and reserving the final sprinkling of chervil until after the lasagne is baked.

❼ Bake in the oven for 25–30 minutes, or until the cheese is melted and lightly browned in places. Serve immediately, with the reserved chervil scattered over.

# Mushroom-ricotta and Sausage Cannelloni

**Cannelloni di Funghi e Salsicche** *Diced, sautéed mushrooms added to ricotta cheese make delicious cannelloni. My secret for easy preparation is to use egg-roll wrappers. If dried porcini are unavailable, you may use ordinary common cultivated mushrooms, about 8–10 ounces, diced and sautéed, in their place.*

SERVES 4

- 3½ oz dried mushrooms, such as porcini
- 1 cup water
- 2 plump, 6-7oz, Italian sausages, roughly chopped
- 5–10 fresh common cultivated mushrooms, diced
- 5 garlic cloves, chopped
- 1½ cups ricotta cheese
- 6 Tbsp freshly shredded Parmesan cheese
- 1 egg, lightly beaten
- salt and ground black pepper, to taste
- several pinches of thyme and/or rosemary, as desired
- 8 egg-roll wrappers, approx. 6-8in. x 6-8in. or fresh pasta
- 2 lb fresh ripe tomatoes or 21 oz canned tomatoes with their juice, diced
- 6 oz mozzarella cheese, shredded
- 1-1½ Tbsp olive oil
- several handfuls fresh basil leaves, roughly torn

**Preparation: 20-30 minutes**

**Cooking time : 30 minutes**

❶ Place the dried mushrooms and the water in a saucepan and bring to a boil. Reduce the heat and simmer for about 5 minutes, then cover, and leave to plump up. When softened, remove the mushrooms from the pan and squeeze, saving the liquid. Roughly chop the mushrooms and strain the mushroom liquid.

❷ Meanwhile, cook the sausages with the fresh mushrooms until lightly browned in spots. Remove from the heat and mix with the garlic, rehydrated mushrooms, ricotta cheese, half the shredded Parmesan cheese, the egg, salt and pepper, and thyme and/or rosemary.

❸ Preheat a 375°F oven. Place several tablespoons of this mixture onto one edge of each pasta square, then roll each into a cylinder. Layer in the bottom of a 9- × 12-inch baking dish.

❹ Pour the diced tomatoes over the top, along with the mushroom liquid, then sprinkle with the mozzarella and remaining Parmesan cheese, and drizzle the olive oil over the top. Bake in the oven for 35–40 minutes, until the pasta is cooked, the liquid absorbed, and the cheese melted. Let stand a few moments, then serve, with the torn basil leaves scattered over.

# Mixed Mushroom Dumplings

*with Wild Mushroom and Chipotle Salsa*

*This cross-cultural dish of mushroom dumplings takes a walk on the wild side with its accompanying Wild Mushroom and Chipotle Salsa (see page 126). For a more sedate, classically European dish, serve it with Mushroom Jus (see page 127) instead.*

SERVES 4

- 25 g/1 oz mixed dried mushrooms, including trompettes de la mort, porcini, mousserons, shiitakes, morels and chanterelles
- 225 g/8 oz cottage cheese or ricotta cheese
- 2 small eggs, lightly beaten
- a few gratings of nutmeg
- 1–2 pinches fresh thyme leaves
- salt and ground black pepper, to taste
- 6 heaped tablespoons freshly grated Parmesan cheese, plus a little extra
- 6 heaped tablespoons self-raising flour, plus extra for rolling dumplings in
- a drizzle of olive oil or a little butter, to finish

**Preparation: 20-30 minutes**
**Cooking time : 25-30 minutes**

❶ Place the mushrooms in a saucepan with 225 ml/8 fl oz water to cover. Bring to the boil, reduce the heat and simmer until the mushrooms are tender, about 5 minutes. Leave to stand in the hot water for about 15 minutes, then squeeze tightly, letting the juices drip back into the liquid.

❷ Roughly chop the mushrooms, then combine them with the cottage or ricotta cheese, the egg, nutmeg, thyme, and salt and pepper, the Parmesan and self-raising flour. The mixture should be thick and slightly stiff. Roll into 12 balls, rolling each in flour to form firm balls.

❸ Preheat a 200–220°C/400°–425°F/gas mark 6–7 oven or a hot grill. Bring a pan of salted water to the boil, reduce the heat and gently lower in the dumplings one at a time. The water should be gently boiling. The dumplings will fall to the bottom and quickly pop up again.

❹ Cover and cook gently over medium-low heat for 5–7 minutes. When cooked, take them out of the water and arrange them in a baking dish, preferably a ceramic one. Drizzle the top with olive oil, or dot with butter, and sprinkle with Parmesan cheese.

❺ Bake for 10 minutes or grill for about 5 minutes, or long enough to brown the dumplings. Serve the hot dumplings with a few spoonfuls of Mushroom and Chipotle Salsa.

*pasta*

Wild and cultivated mushrooms make marvellous flavours to sauce or stew most any meats, poultry or fish. Many of the following sauces could be interchangeable: try using pork in place of prawns, or chicken in place of veal anywhere.

# Fillet Steak Sautéed with Mushrooms

## in Soured Cream Sauce 'alla Russe'

*This lush, creamy, nutmeg-scented sauce, studded with chunks of barely cooked mushrooms and rare fillet steak, is one of my oldest favourite Russian-inspired mushroom dishes.*

SERVES 4

- 1 large onion
- 40–65 g/1½–2½ oz butter
- 225 g/8 oz common cultivated mushrooms, cut into big chunks or quartered
- 3 garlic cloves, chopped
- 225–350 g/8–12 oz fillet steak, cut into bite-size pieces
- 1 Tbsp flour
- 175 ml/6 fl oz each dry white wine and beef stock
- 225 ml/8 fl oz crème fraîche or soured cream
- a generous pinch each freshly grated nutmeg and dried basil
- salt and black pepper, to taste
- a few drops lemon juice, if needed

**Preparation: 15-20 minutes**
**Cooking time : 15-20 minutes**

❶ Lightly sauté the onion in half the butter until softened, then remove from the pan and set aside. Using any butter that is left behind, or adding a little extra if needed, raise the heat and sauté the mushrooms and garlic in several batches until lightly browned but not cooked through. Place with the onion, along with any juices.

❷ Very quickly brown the meat to seal, letting it only sear and not cook through. Set aside on a plate.

❸ Melt any remaining butter in the same pan and sprinkle with the flour, letting it cook for a few minutes. Take off the heat, pour in the wine and stock, and stir well to let it thicken slightly. Boil to reduce to a concentrated sauce, then remove from the heat. Add the reserved mushrooms and onion, and crème fraîche or soured cream. Heat gently, then add nutmeg, basil, salt and pepper.

❹ Add the reserved steak and heat until just warmed through. Taste, and add lemon juice to balance the richness of the sauce, and more salt and pepper if necessary. Serve with spaetzel or brown rice.

# Rosemary-roasted Veal

## or Pork with Catalan-style Braised Mushrooms

*Braised mushrooms, Catalan-style, added to the pan juices makes a luscious sauce for roasted meat, whether you choose veal or pork. Almost any mushrooms are delicious, but you must use fresh tomatoes—canned won't do.*

SERVES 6

- 1.25 kg/2½ lb boned, lean veal or pork roasted (rolled, by the butcher, and tied, is excellent and will help it stay neat during roasting)
- several sprigs fresh rosemary
- 10–12 garlic cloves, half cut into slivers, half chopped
- salt and ground black pepper, to taste
- 4 Tbsp olive oil
- 2 carrots, diced
- 10 garlic cloves, left whole but peeled
- 1 large onion, chopped
- 3 fresh ripe tomatoes, grated and skins discarded
- 450 g/1 lb mixed fresh wild mushrooms, or cultivated common mushrooms mixed with a few handfuls of dried mixed exotic mushrooms
- Dry white wine or stock, if needed

**Preparation: 30 minutes**
**Cooking time : 3 hours**

❶ Preheat a 180°C/350°F/gas mark 4 oven. Make incisions all over the meat. Into each one insert a sprig of rosemary that you have dipped into a little salt and a sliver of garlic. Stud the whole roast, then rub it with olive oil. Scatter the carrots, whole garlic cloves and a few rosemary sprigs on the base of a roasting tin. Place the roast on a roasting rack, if you have one, or on the base of the tin. Place in the oven for 1 hour 15 minutes.

❷ Meanwhile, sauté the onion slowly in the remaining olive oil, sprinkling with salt to draw out the juices, until soft, about 20 minutes. Stir in the chopped garlic, then add the tomatoes and raise the heat, cooking until the tomatoes melt into the onions, and the oil begins to separate. Add the mushrooms, reduce the heat and cook over medium-low heat, stirring occasionally, until the mushrooms are cooked through. The moisture from the fresh mushrooms should rehydrate any dried ones used, but

if it doesn't, add a little stock or dry white wine to the pan, and boil until the mushrooms rehydrate.

❸ When the mushrooms are tender, season with salt and pepper, and set aside until the meat is ready. (A meat thermometer is useful here so that you can gauge the inside of the meat without cutting into it.)

❹ Remove the cooked veal or pork from its tin, pour off any fat from the surface but save any juices, then add a few tablespoons of wine or stock. Place on the cooker and scrape the base of the tin. Add the braised mushrooms and warm through, then set aside and keep warm.

❺ Slice the roast, then serve each portion with a few spoonfuls of the mushroom sauce.

*poultry, meat & fish*

# Sautéed Mixed Mushrooms

### *with Bacon, Chervil and Watercress or Mâche (Corn salad or lamb's lettuce)*

*This bistro-style dish is simple to prepare and marvellous for a winter supper. Any firm fleshy flavourful mushroom is fine; oyster mushrooms, chanterelles, trompette de la mort, and perhaps a few slices of porcini.*

- 450–675 g/1–1½ lb mixed fresh mushrooms, cut into bite-size pieces
- 40–50 g/1½–2 oz butter, or half butter and half olive oil
- 1 shallot, chopped
- 175 g/6 oz smoked bacon or good ham, such as prosciutto or jamon, cut into bite-size pieces
- 1 garlic clove, chopped
- a handful of watercress or mâche, roughly chopped
- 1 Tbsp chopped fresh chervil, tarragon, parsley or a combination
- pain levain or similar country-style bread, to serve

**Preparation: 10 minutes**

**Cooking time : 10-15 minutes**

❶ Lightly sauté the mushrooms in the butter, or butter and olive oil, with the shallot and bacon or ham. When the mushrooms and bacon are browned, stir in the garlic and cook for a few moments more. Serve garnished with the tufts of watercress or mâche, which will wilt slightly, and chopped herbs. Tuck in with a chunk of pain levain.

# Daube aux Champignons Sauvages

**Lamb stew with wild mushrooms** Once you've browned the meat and added everything else, the stew takes care of itself until you add the wild mushrooms. I like to add a few dried mushrooms into the pot along with the wine to boost the mushroom flavours and aromas.

SERVES 6

- 1 carrot, chopped
- 2 leeks, chopped
- 3–4 Tbsp olive oil
- about 1.5 kg/3–3½ lb boneless lamb joint, such as a shoulder, with enough fat to keep it moist, cut into bite-size chunks
- salt, ground black pepper and thyme, to taste
- flour, for dredging
- 400 g/14 oz tomatoes, fresh or canned, diced
- 3 bay leaves
- 225 ml/8 fl oz beef stock
- 1 bottle robust red wine, such as a Merlot or Zinfandel
- 2–3 Tbsp dried wild mushrooms
- 1 garlic bulb, separated into cloves and peeled
- 350 g/12 oz mixed fresh wild mushrooms such as oyster, chanterelles, trompettes de la mort, mousserons, porcini, with a handful of common cultivated mushrooms, all cut into bite-size pieces
- 3–5 garlic cloves, chopped
- 1–2 Tbsp chopped fresh parsley

**Preparation: 20 minutes**

**Cooking time : 3½-4 hours**

❶ Sauté the carrot and leeks in the olive oil until softened, then place in a heavy-based casserole dish.

❷ Season the meat with salt, pepper and thyme, then dredge with the flour, shaking off the excess. In the same pan used for the vegetables, brown the meat in a little olive oil for a few minutes, working in small batches so as not to crowd the pan. Place the meat into the casserole with the sautéed vegetables.

❸ Add the tomatoes, the bay leaves, beef stock, wine, dried mushrooms and whole garlic cloves to the casserole. Bring to the boil, reduce the heat, then either simmer very gently on top of the cooker or bake in a 170°C/325°F/gas mark 3 oven for about 3 hours.

❹ Remove from the cooker or oven and leave to stand a few moments. Skim off the fat that has accumulated at the top. If the sauce is thin, pour it off into a saucepan and boil it to reduce. It might need 10–20 minutes, depending on how liquid it is.

❺ Meanwhile, sauté the fresh mushrooms in a tablespoon or two of the olive oil and season with salt and pepper, and the chopped garlic. Add to the meat, along with the mushroom juices.

❻ When the sauce has reduced, pour it back into the casserole with the meat and mushrooms. Return to the oven or the cooker for about 15 minutes. Serve with the chopped parsley scattered over.

VARIATION:

Instead of lamb, this is an excellent dish for beef in the classic boeuf bourguignon style.

*poultry, meat & fish*

71

# Poulet aux Cèpes

**Roasted garlic chicken with porcini, cream, pink peppercorns and chervil** *A golden brown chicken, its flesh infused with the scent of its garlic stuffing, is served in a creamy sauce rich with porcini, and sprinkled with pink peppercorns and chervil.*

*If chervil is unavailable, use tarragon, chives or parsley. If porcini are not available, use a mixed mushroom combination.*

SERVES 4

- 1 chicken, about 1 kg/2¼ lb
- salt and ground black pepper, to taste
- 3 Tbsp soft butter, duck fat or olive oil
- ½ lemon, cut into several chunks
- 2 garlic bulbs, separated into cloves but left whole and unpeeled
- 3 Tbsp fresh tarragon or thyme
- 25 g/1 oz dried porcini
- 225 ml/8 fl oz hot, but not boiling, water
- 2 shallots, chopped
- 225 ml/8 fl oz dry white wine
- 225 ml/8 oz chicken stock
- 225 g/8 oz crème fraîche or double cream
- 1 Tbsp pink peppercorns
- 2–3 Tbsp chopped fresh chervil

**Preparation: 15 minutes**
**Cooking time : 1½ hours**

❶ Preheat a 170°C/325°F/gas mark 3 oven. Place the chicken in a roasting tin and rub its insides and outsides with salt, pepper, and about half the butter, duck fat or olive oil. Fill its insides with the lemon chunks, about half of the whole garlic cloves, and the tarragon or thyme. Scatter the rest of the garlic cloves around the chicken.

❷ Roast the chicken for about an hour, or until golden brown and just tender. Remove from the oven and leave to stand for 10 minutes to rest before carving. Meanwhile, make the porcini sauce.

❸ Rehydrate the dried porcini by putting them in a bowl with the hot water. Leave to stand for 30 minutes, remove, squeeze, and save the mushroom liquid.

❹ Lightly sauté the mushrooms in the remaining butter, duck fat or olive oil, with the chopped shallots. Add the mushroom liquid, wine and stock, and reduce over high heat to about 225 ml/8 fl oz in total. Add the crème fraîche or cream, reduce the heat and simmer until thickened, about 20 minutes.

❺ When the chicken has roasted and stood for 10 minutes, carve it and keep warm.

❻ Carefully skim the fat from the pan juices, then stir the warm mushroom sauce into the tin, scraping the base to release all the rich crusty bits. If the base of the tin is too crusty, pour a little stock or white wine in first, cook through and deglaze to release the bits, and then add the mushroom sauce.

❼ Serve the chicken surrounded by the roasted garlic cloves and blanketed by the porcini sauce. Scatter over pink peppercorns and chervil, and serve immediately.

TIP:

Save the chicken carcass to make stock to use in soups and sauces.

# Poulet aux Morilles

**Pan-sautéed chicken with morel mushrooms** *You can make this with all breasts or all dark meat, and similarly, you can roast or grill the chicken pieces before adding them to your sauce if you prefer not to sauté.*

SERVES 4–6

- 25 g/1 oz dried morels
- 450 ml/¾ pint water
- 1 chicken, about 1.5 kg/3 lb, cut in serving pieces
- salt and ground black pepper, to taste
- 2 Tbsp olive oil
- 25 g/1 oz butter, preferably sweet
- 3–5 shallots, chopped
- 3 Tbsp brandy or Marsala
- 225 g/8 oz crème fraîche or soured cream, stirred with a few tablespoons of double cream and a squeeze of lemon juice
- 2 Tbsp chopped fresh chervil, parsley or snipped fresh chives

---

**Preparation: 30-40 minutes**

**Cooking time : 1 hour**

---

❶ Place the morels and the water in a saucepan and bring to the boil. Cook over medium heat until tender, and the liquid turns brown and thickens. After 20–30 minutes, it should have reduced by about half. Remove from the heat, take the morels out of the liquid and place on a plate. Strain the liquid through muslin or pour off the top and leave behind the grit.

❷ Rub the chicken pieces with salt and pepper, then sauté them in the olive oil and butter until lightly browned. You will need to do this in batches. Remove to a casserole or plate as you cook them.

❸ When the chicken pieces are all browned, pour off all the fat except for about 1 tablespoon, then sauté the shallots. Return the chicken to the pan, then pour in the brandy or the Marsala, taking care to avert your face when it flames. Remember not to pour it straight from the bottle. Mix the crème fraîche or soured cream with the mushroom liquid and mushrooms, and add to the pan.

❹ Cook over low heat for about 25 minutes, or until the chicken is cooked through. You may like to keep the white meat portions out of the pan for the first 10 minutes, since the dark meat requires longer cooking, and the white meat will overcook and become dry if left on the heat too long.

❺ Serve each portion with a few spoonfuls of sauce and a sprinkling of fresh herbs.

*poultry, meat & fish*

# Poulet aux Champignons, Sauce à la Crème

**Chicken breasts, stuffed with wild mushroom duxelles, in cream sauce** *The light creamy flesh of chicken breast is the perfect vehicle for enjoying the strong foresty scent and taste of wild mushrooms.*

SERVES 4

- 75 g/3 oz mixed dried mushrooms
- 350 ml/12 fl oz water
- 4 boned chicken breast halves
- 2 shallots, chopped
- 3 garlic cloves, chopped
- salt and ground black pepper, to taste
- juice of ¼ lemon
- 2 Tbsp dry white wine
- 1 Tbsp olive oil
- 225 ml/8 fl oz chicken stock
- 40 g/1½ oz butter
- 100 ml/4 fl oz single cream
- 1 Tbsp each chopped fresh chervil and snipped fresh chives, to garnish (optional)

**Preparation: 20-30 minutes**

**Cooking time : 15 minutes**

❶ Place the mushrooms and water in a saucepan and bring to the boil. Reduce the heat and simmer for about 15 minutes. Remove them from the liquid and chop roughly.

❷ Cut a pocket in each chicken piece, then marinate with half the shallots, garlic, salt and pepper, lemon juice, white wine and olive oil. Leave to stand while you prepare the duxelle filling and sauce.

❸ Strain the mushroom liquid and reduce to about 100 ml/4 fl oz. Add the chicken stock and remaining wine, and reduce to about 225 ml/8 fl oz until thin but saucelike. Set aside.

❹ Sauté the mushrooms with the remaining shallots and garlic in 25 g/1 oz of the butter. Add a spoonful or two of the sauce, then continue to cook the mushrooms until they form a dryish filling. Remove from the heat and season.

❺ Remove the chicken breasts, saving the marinade, and stuff with a few spoonfuls of the mushroom mixture. Seal with cocktail sticks. Set aside.

❻ Heat the pan, add the remaining butter, then sauté the chicken breasts on each side for 3 minutes.

❼ Remove from the pan and pour in any remaining marinade, the sauce and the cream. Stir for about 5 minutes.

❽ Serve the chicken breasts, with their sauce, garnished with the chervil and chives.

# Chicken or Turkey 'Bitkies'

Minced chicken or turkey is mixed with shredded raw mushrooms in this Russian-inspired dish, then seasoned with parsley, tarragon, capers and lots and lots of garlic. The patties are then fried and served with a creamy mushroom sauce.

SERVES 4–6

- 1 kg/2¼ lb minced chicken or turkey
- 10–15 garlic cloves, roughly chopped
- 100 g/4 oz fresh breadcrumbs
- 2 eggs, lightly beaten
- 1–2 Tbsp chopped fresh parsley, plus extra to garnish
- 1 Tbsp chopped fresh tarragon (optional)
- 2 tsp capers
- 350 g/12 oz fresh mushrooms
- salt and ground black pepper, to taste
- oil or butter, for sautéeing
- 5 shallots, chopped
- 100 ml/4 fl oz dry white wine or stock, or a combination
- 100 ml/4 fl oz single cream
- 225 g/8 oz crème fraîche or soured cream
- a squeeze of lemon, if needed

**Preparation: 10 minutes**
**Cooking time : 15-20 minutes**

❶ Combine the chicken or turkey, garlic, breadcrumbs, eggs, parsley, tarragon and capers. Shred about 100 g/4 oz of the mushrooms. Add to mixture, season with salt and pepper, then form into patties.

❷ Brown the patties, in batches, in a heavy-based frying pan in a little oil or butter, taking care that they do not fall apart. As they are cooked, transfer to a plate or pan, and keep warm.

❸ Pour off all the fat except for about a tablespoon, and in this lightly sauté the shallots and remaining mushrooms until softened. Then pour in the wine and/or stock, and reduce to a few tablespoons. Stir in the cream and crème fraîche or soured cream, taste for seasoning and return the patties to the sauce. Season with salt, pepper and, if needed, a squeeze of lemon. Sprinkle with parsley and serve immediately.

# Morel and Chicken Pie

For this dish, other mushrooms are fine in place of the morels—porcini, especially so, for a foresty mixture. And, you can vary the vegetables too—leeks or asparagus, tiny blanched turnips, or new potatoes are all good choices. Sweetbreads or chicken livers also make good additions.

SERVES 4

- 40 g/1½ oz dried morel mushrooms
- 225 ml/8 fl oz water or stock
- 3 shallots, chopped
- 2 garlic cloves, chopped
- 40 g/1½ oz butter
- 3 Tbsp brandy
- salt and white pepper, to taste
- 2 chicken thighs or dark meat, boned and diced
- 2 boneless chicken breasts, cut into bite-size pieces
- 2 Tbsp flour
- 5 Tbsp double cream
- a grating of nutmeg
- 675 g/1½ lb puff pastry

**Preparation: 40-50 minutes**
**Cooking time : 30-45 minutes**

❶ Rehydrate the mushrooms in the water or stock in a saucepan. Bring to the boil, then simmer over low heat for about 5 minutes. Leave to soak until cool enough to handle, about 20 minutes. Squeeze out the mushrooms, reserving the liquid. Chop the mushrooms and set aside. Strain the liquid and set aside.

❷ Lightly sauté the chopped mushrooms with the shallots and garlic in about half the butter, until the mushrooms are just tender and lightly browned. Add the brandy, taking care to avert your face in case it flames, and cook over high heat for a few moments. Season with salt and pepper, and set aside.

❸ Season the chicken meat with salt and pepper, then toss it in flour. Lightly brown in the remaining butter. Do not cook the meat through, only let it turn light golden on the outside, then remove it from the pan.

❹ Preheat a 200°C/400°F/gas mark 6 oven. Into the pan add the mushroom liquid, reduce by about half, then add the cream, and pour in any liquid that has accumulated from the mushrooms. Cook over high heat until the mixture thickens again. Season with the nutmeg, salt and pepper.

▲ Morel and Chicken Pie

❺ Combine the sauce with the mushrooms and chicken, then pour into either one large or four individual pie dishes.

❻ Roll out the pastry and cover the pie(s), sealing the edges of the crust to the pie dish. Bake in the oven for about 25 minutes, or until the top of the pastry is golden or lightly brown and crisply puffy. Serve immediately.

TIP:
Instead of just dried morels, use 50 g/2 oz mixed dried mushrooms, or 225 g/8 oz common cultivated mushrooms with 25 g/1 oz dried morels, or 275 g/10 oz fresh morels or other wild mushrooms. If you don't use the dried variety, you will need 225 ml/8 fl oz stock for the sauce.

# Saumon aux Trompettes de la Mort

**Salmon with trompettes de la mort** *Trompettes de la mort translate as 'trumpets of death' from the French. They are thus named for their blackish colour, not because of any danger! They are not only safe, they are delectable, a favourite in the Jura mountains in the west of France where they are layered with potatoes for spectacular gratins.*

*Their black colour looks particularly fine with the pale pink of salmon. If you can find black chanterelles or trompettes de la mort fresh, do use them and, if you cannot, use dried ones. Yellow chanterelles can be combined with the black chanterelle or trompettes de la mort, and will taste lovely but not look so striking as the all-black.*

SERVES 4

- 675 g/1½ lb salmon fillets
- salt and ground black pepper, to taste
- juice of ¼ lemon
- 350 g/12 oz fresh trompettes de la mort, black chanterelles or chanterelles, or use 25 g/1 oz dried trompettes de la mort or black chanterelles
- 50 g/2 oz butter
- 4 shallots, chopped
- 1 garlic clove, chopped
- 100 ml/4 fl oz each dry white wine and fish stock
- 4 Tbsp double cream or crème fraîche

**Preparation: 15 minutes**
**Cooking time : 15-20 minutes**

❶ Sprinkle the salmon with salt, pepper and lemon juice. Set aside while you cook the mushrooms.

❷ Cut the mushrooms into bite-size pieces. If using dried mushrooms, place them in a saucepan with the white wine and bring to the boil. Reduce the heat, simmer for about 5 minutes, then leave to stand and plump up. Remove from the wine and squeeze dry, saving the mushroom liquid. Cut the mushrooms into bite-size pieces and set aside. Strain the wine and set aside.

❸ Melt half the butter and sauté the fresh or rehydrated mushrooms, shallots and garlic until softened. Season with salt and pepper, then add the wine and fish stock. Bring to the boil, cook over high heat until reduced by about half, then stir in the cream or crème fraîche. Taste for seasoning and set aside to keep warm.

❹ Melt the remaining butter and reserve a tablespoon. Cook the bottom (skin side) of the salmon fillets. Brush the tops with the reserved melted butter, then place under the grill to cook the top, 1–2 minutes.

❺ Reheat the sauce, if necessary, and spoon it onto warmed plates, then top each with a portion of the sautéed salmon and serve.

*poultry, meat & fish*

# Prawns and Scallops with Mushrooms

## in Spicy Thai Sauce

*You can make this with just prawns or just scallops instead of both, or with chicken breast, or tofu instead. Often I expand the dish with more and more vegetables, depending on what is available.*

*Serve in a soup bowl with a spoonful of rice or a tangle of rice noodles alongside, to soak up the rich, spicy sauce.*

SERVES 4

- 10 dried mixed mushrooms such as shiitake, or Chinese black mushrooms
- 10 each dried small and large black fungus (tree cloud)
- 450 ml/¾ pint stock
- 5 shallots, chopped
- 5 garlic cloves, chopped
- 3 Tbsp vegetable oil
- ½ tsp each turmeric and curry powder
- 1 tsp ground coriander
- 1 Tbsp chopped fresh root ginger
- 1 medium-hot fresh red chilli such as jalapeño, thinly sliced
- 1 carrot, sliced diagonally
- ¼ aubergine, cut into small bite-size pieces or diced
- ¼ red pepper, chopped
- 100–150 g/4–5 oz common cultivated mushrooms, cut into bite-size pieces
- 3–4 kaffir lime leaves, fresh or dried
- 10–12 spears very thin asparagus, cut into bite-size lengths
- 90 g/3½ oz creamed coconut, in small pieces
- 8 each large prawns and scallops, trimmed and halved or quartered
- juice of ½ lime, or as desired

**Preparation: 15-20 minutes**
**Cooking time : 15-20 minutes**

❶ Place the shiitake or Chinese black mushrooms and two types of black fungus in a saucepan with the stock. Bring to the boil, reduce the heat and simmer for about 5 minutes. Cover and leave while you prepare the rest of the dish.

❷ Lightly sauté the shallots and garlic in the vegetable oil until softened, then sprinkle in the turmeric, curry powder, coriander, ginger, chilli, carrot, aubergine, red pepper and the rest of the mushrooms, and cook until the vegetables are half tender, about 5 minutes.

❸ Remove the rehydrated mushrooms and fungus from the stock. Cut the large black fungus into smaller pieces, leaving the smaller fungus and the mushrooms whole. Strain the mushroom liquid.

❹ Pour the strained liquid into the sautéeing vegetables, along with the lime leaves, and cook a few minutes together. Add the rehydrated mushrooms and fungus, the asparagus, prawns and scallops. Stir well but gently, and add the creamed coconut, tossing gently over medium heat until the coconut has emulsified into the sauce. The asparagus and seafood should be just cooked through. Serve immediately, with a squeeze of lime.

VARIATION:

Thai Curry with Tomatoes and Flour Tortillas

Add 5–8 ripe tomatoes, diced, to the simmering vegetables, canned is fine. Serve with warmed flour tortillas to dip into the spicy mixture and to wrap up pieces of vegetables and seafood.

# Rizhskoye Telnoye

*Russian Fish stuffed with mushrooms in a creamy sauce*

*This dish is classic French-inspired Russian, full of aristocratic flavours and luxury ingredients.*

SERVES 4

**For the stuffed fish fillets**
- 4 thin fish fillets such as flounder or plaice, about 150 g/6 oz each
- salt and ground black pepper
- 250–300 g/10–12 oz common cultivated mushrooms, brown or white, or field mushrooms, chopped
- 3 shallots, chopped
- 1 garlic clove, chopped
- 2 Tbsp chopped fresh parsley
- 4 Tbsp butter
- 3–4 Tbsp double cream, crème fraîche, or sour cream
- a few gratings of nutmeg
- 225 ml/8 fl oz each fish or chicken stock and dry white wine or dry white vermouth

**For the sauce**
- 1 Tbsp butter
- 1 Tbsp flour
- poaching liquid from above, adding more stock or wine/vermouth if needed
- 112 ml/4 fl oz double cream, crème fraîche, or sour cream
- salt and ground black pepper
- 1 egg yolk
- juice of ½ lemon

- 1 Tbsp snipped fresh chives
- 3–4 Tbsp shredded Gruyère and Parmesan cheese

**Preparation: 30 minutes**
**Cooking time : 15 minutes**

❶ Place the fish fillets between sheets of grease proof paper and pound them gently into flat escalopes. Season, and set aside.

❷ Sauté the mushrooms, shallots, garlic, and parsley until lightly browned, about 10–15 minutes. Add the cream, crème fraîche, or sour cream. Cook over high heat to form a thickish paste. Season with nutmeg, salt, and pepper.

❸ Spoon one quarter of the mushrooms onto each fillet. Roll up, and close with toothpicks.

❹ Place the stuffed fish fillets in a heavy-based frying pan along with the stock and wine or vermouth. Bring to the boil, then cook over very low heat until the fish is no longer opaque on the outside and barely cooked through.

❺ Remove the stuffed fish fillets to a gratin baking dish. Any bits of mushroom or fish that have fallen into the poaching liquid will enrich it. If too much stuffing has fallen out, simply spoon it back in.

❻ Boil the poaching liquid until it reduces to 280 ml/10 fl oz, 7–10 minutes.

❼ Preheat a 400°F oven. Make the sauce; melt the butter, sprinkle in the flour, and let cook a minute or two. Remove from the heat and stir in the hot reduced stock all at once, then return to the heat and stir together until thickened. In a bowl, stir together the egg yolk and cream, crème fraîche, or sour cream, lemon juice, and chives.

❽ Stir a little of the hot sauce into this, then stir this back into the hot sauce, and pour it over the stuffed fish fillets. Sprinkle with cheese, then place in the oven and bake about 10 minutes or until fish is hot and the top is crisp and lightly browned. Serve hot.

Almost every mushroom is delicious with eggs: you can count on a buttery little scramble to bring out the best in your fungi. Tuck sautéed mushrooms into an omelette, or splash them into a sauce and lavish them onto poached eggs. If you are ever in doubt about what to do with a cache of extravagant fungi, you can't go far wrong with a basketful of fresh eggs and a frying pan.

# Omelette aux Mousserons

**Omelette with mousserons** This omelette from southwestern France has a real 'gout d'automne', the flavour of autumn, with its woody mushrooms. If you do not have mousserons, use any flavourful mushrooms, especially porcini, or a mixture of common cultivated brown mushrooms mixed with a few tablespoons of delicious dried mushrooms.

Though in southwestern France they would traditionally use the fat from a duck or goose for this dish, I tend to favour olive oil or butter.

SERVES 4

- 350 g/12 oz mousserons, diced
- 1 slice (about 50 g/2 oz) prosciutto, jamon or other strong-flavoured raw ham, diced
- 3 garlic cloves, chopped
- 1–2 Tbsp chopped fresh parsley
- 2–3 Tbsp olive oil or butter
- salt and ground black pepper, to taste
- 8–10 eggs, lightly beaten
- 2–4 Tbsp milk

**Preparation: 20-25 minutes**

**Cooking time : 10 minutes**

❶ Lightly sauté the mushrooms together with the ham, garlic and parsley, in about half the olive oil or butter, until just tender. Season with salt and pepper, and set aside.

❷ Combine the eggs with the milk.

❸ Heat a small omelette pan for four individual omelettes or a large pan for one large or two medium-size omelettes. For four individual omelettes, add a teaspoon or two of olive oil or butter to the hot pan, then pour in a quarter of the egg mixture. Cook a few moments, as for a rolled omelette, then spoon in a quarter of the mushroom mixture. Roll the sides over and roll the omelette out of the pan.

Repeat with the remaining ingredients. For one large omelette, do the same, using all the egg and filling in one go. For two medium-size omelettes, do the same, using half the mixtures for each. Serve immediately.

# Oeufs en Cocotte aux Champignons

**Eggs baked in a ramekin with cream and sautéed mushrooms**

*Plump eggs rest on top of a bed of sautéed mushrooms, and more or less poach in the oven, nestled beneath a cream and cheese topping.*

*Sometimes I use the sauce for poached eggs rather than making individual ramekins.*

SERVES 4
- 5 shallots, chopped
- 3 garlic cloves, chopped
- 40 g/1½ oz butter
- 100 g/4 oz fresh mushrooms, preferably a mixture of wild or exotic, roughly chopped or diced
- 3 Tbsp Cognac or brandy
- 3 Tbsp dry white wine
- 225 g/8 oz crème fraîche or double cream
- a grating of nutmeg
- salt, to taste
- 1 tsp fresh thyme
- 4 or 8 eggs, depending on whether each person will have one or two
- 175 g/6 oz mild cheese, such as comte, Gruyère, Emmental or a combination of any of these, plus Parmesan, grated

**Preparation: 10 minutes**
**Cooking time : 30 minutes**

❶ Preheat a 200°C/400°F/gas mark 6 oven. Lightly sauté the shallots and garlic in the butter, then add the mushrooms, and cook until lightly browned, about 10 minutes. Pour in the Cognac or brandy (averting your face as you do), cook over high heat until evaporated, then add the wine and cook a few minutes more. Stir in the crème fraîche or cream, the nutmeg, salt and thyme, and set aside.

❷ Into the base of four individual ramekins, place a tablespoon or so of the mushrooms. Top with one or two eggs slid right on top of the mushrooms without scrambling them in any way, then sprinkle with the cheese.

❸ Bake in the oven for 10–15 minutes, or long enough to cook the eggs through. Serve immediately.

# Oeufs en Meurette aux Champignons

**Eggs in red wine sauce with braised mushrooms** *Poached eggs, blanketed in red wine and mushroom sauce, make a delectable dish for either brunch or a bistro-style supper. The dish is vegetarian as is, but for omnivores, garnish with a handful of crisply browned diced bacon or pancetta.*

SERVES 4
- 1 bottle red wine, such as a Côtes de Rhône, Cahors, Cabernet or Zinfandel
- 450 ml/¾ pint stock
- 3 cloves
- 1 bay leaf
- a few sprigs fresh thyme
- 1 leek, including the green part, diced
- 3 garlic cloves, roughly chopped
- 1 celery stick, diced
- 2 carrots, chopped
- 1 Tbsp tomato purée
- 50 g/2 oz butter
- 225 g/8 oz mixed fresh mushrooms
- 3 Tbsp flour
- a few drops balsamic vinegar
- 4 or 8 eggs, depending on whether each person will have one or two
- 1–2 tsp vinegar for poaching

**Preparation: 20-30 minutes**

**Cooking time : 1½-2 hours**

❶ Combine the wine, stock, cloves, bay leaf, thyme, leek, garlic, celery and carrots in a saucepan and bring to the boil. Cook over medium-high heat for about an hour, or until reduced by about half. The vegetables should be very, very tender by now. If they are not, continue cooking until they are. Mix in the tomato purée, then pour the sauce through a strainer, pushing on the solids to extract all the juices, leaving behind only the fibrous parts which you should discard.

❷ Melt the butter in a heavy-based frying pan and sauté the mushrooms until lightly browned. Then sprinkle with the flour and add the wine sauce, stirring as you pour it in. You may need to transfer this to a large casserole or heavy-based saucepan to accommodate all the mushrooms and sauce.

❸ Simmer the mixture for about 30 minutes, letting the mushrooms braise in the sauce.

❹ When you are ready to serve, poach the eggs in just simmering water to which you have added the vinegar. Do not salt the water; that makes the eggs ragged, whereas vinegar holds them together.

❺ Lift the eggs from their poaching liquid, dry on absorbent kitchen paper or a clean tea towel, then place on warmed plates, and serve with the mushroom wine sauce. Eat immediately.

TIP:

I like to include oyster mushrooms, chanterelles, trompettes de la mort and porcini in this recipe. If you like, you can add some common cultivated mushrooms as well.

Wild and tamed mushrooms taste wonderful with all manner of grains. The grains seem to balance the strong earthy flavours of the fungi delightfully, whether they are light rices stirred into risotti, hefty buckwheat or barley of Eastern Europe, or fine long grain rices of the Far East.

*grains*

# Kasha-varnichkes

## with Wild Mushrooms and Sautéed Onions

*This tastes of childhood dinners prepared by Russian or Polish mamas and grandmas, even if you yourself have been nowhere near Eastern Europe.*

*Kasha is utterly delicious eaten with nearly any kind of sautéed mushroom. I like to stuff pasta with kasha and fried onions sometimes, and serve it in a sauce of sautéed mushrooms with soured cream and a scent of nutmeg.*

*This dish is delicious just as is, though meatballs in a little soured cream sauce alongside would make a feast fit for a czar, as you might say!*

SERVES 4

- 225 g/8 oz kasha
- 175 g/6 oz butterfly shaped pasta or other short noodle shapes
- 25 g/1 oz dried porcini or other wild mushroom mix
- 600 ml/1 pint chicken or vegetable stock
- 3 onions, chopped or sliced
- 3–5 Tbsp vegetable oil
- 25–40 g/1–1½ oz butter
- 275–350 g/10–12 oz common cultivated mushrooms, sliced
- soured cream or yogurt, to serve (optional)

**Preparation: 20-30 minutes**

**Cooking time : 45 minutes**

❶ Lightly toast the kasha in a heavy-based, ungreased saucepan until it smells toasty and turns light nutty brown. Remove from the heat and set aside.

❷ Cook the pasta in rapidly boiling salted water until just tender, then drain well and rinse with cold water. Drain again and set aside.

❸ Simmer the dried mushrooms in the stock for about 15 minutes, or until tender, then remove from the heat. Take the mushrooms out of the liquid and set aside. Strain the liquid and add to the kasha.

❹ Place the kasha on the cooker and bring to the boil. Reduce the heat to low, cover and simmer until the liquid is absorbed, about 15 minutes.

❺ Meanwhile, cook the onions in the oil and butter until softened

and browned, about 15 minutes. Add the rehydrated and cultivated mushrooms, and cook until browned and tender. Season with salt and pepper.

❻ Combine the kasha with the pasta and onion-mushroom mixture. Check for seasoning and serve hot, with soured cream or rich yogurt on the side, if desired.

*Grains*

# Mixed Mushroom Pilaf

SERVES 4

*with Truffle or Porcini Oil*

- 3 shallots, chopped
- 2 garlic cloves, chopped
- 25–40 g/1–1½ oz butter
- 300 g/11 oz long grain rice
- 900 ml/1½ pints chicken or vegetable stock
- 225 g/8 oz mixed fresh or 50–75 g/2–3 oz mixed dried mushrooms, rehydrated and squeezed dry, diced
- a drizzle of truffle oil or 1 Tbsp porcini oil
- 1–2 Tbsp fresh snipped chives

*Lightly butter-toasted grains of rice are perfumed with the foresty scent of mushrooms. This is lovely with scallops of veal or chicken breast lightly cooked over a wood fire, or trout wrapped in grape leaves and bacon, then barbecued.*

---

**Preparation: 15 minutes**

**Cooking time : 20 minutes**

---

❶ In a large saucepan, lightly sauté the shallots and garlic in the butter until softened. Do not brown.

❷ Set aside half the shallot mixture from the pan. Then gently cook the rice in the remaining mixture until golden. Stir in the stock, lower the heat and cover tightly. Cook until the rice is almost tender, about 6–8 minutes.

❸ Meanwhile, place the remaining shallot mixture in a frying pan and sauté the mushrooms in it. When the rice is almost tender and still just slightly soupy, toss in the sautéed mushrooms, cover and continue to cook over low heat 3–4 minutes more, or until the rice grains are just tender.

❹ Fluff the rice up with a fork, then serve immediately, drizzled with the truffle or porcini oil, and with the chives scattered over.

# Polenta al Ragù di Funghi

SERVES 4–6

**Polenta with meaty tomato-mushroom sauce** *Hearty mushrooms enrich this tomatoey sauce for polenta. If you have a couple of Italian sausages, add them to your sauce with, or in place of, the minced beef.*

- 1 onion, chopped
- 1 carrot, chopped
- 1 celery stick, including the leaves, chopped
- 2 Tbsp olive oil
- 5 garlic cloves, roughly chopped
- 2 Tbsp chopped fresh parsley
- 450 g/1 lb lean minced beef
- 3–4 rashers of bacon, diced
- 225 ml/8 fl oz dry red wine
- 225 ml/8 fl oz beef stock
- 50 g/2 oz dried mushrooms,

preferably porcini, broken into small pieces
- 900 g/2 lb fresh ripe tomatoes or 2 × 400-g/14-oz cans tomatoes, diced
- 2 Tbsp tomato purée
- 2 bay leaves
- a pinch of sugar (optional)
- salt and ground black pepper

- 3–5 Tbsp fresh basil leaves, lightly crushed or chopped
- 675 g/1½ lb polenta
- 1.5 litres/2½ pints water, or more if needed
- freshly grated Parmesan cheese, a few gratings of nutmeg and butter as desired, to serve

▲ *Polenta al Ragù di Funghi*

❶ In a large saucepan, sauté the onion, carrot and celery in the olive oil until softened, then stir in the garlic, parsley, beef and bacon. Continue cooking, breaking up the meat with a fork, until it is no longer pink. Pour in the wine and cook over high heat until nearly all the liquid has evaporated.

❷ Add the stock, mushrooms, tomatoes, tomato purée, bay leaves, sugar (if using), salt and pepper and basil leaves. Bring to the boil, then reduce the heat and simmer until the sauce is thickened, about an hour.

❸ Meanwhile cook the polenta. Mix the polenta with 100 ml/ 4 fl oz cold water and let stand a few minutes. Bring the remaining water to the boil, then add a pinch of salt and, using a wooden spoon, slowly stir in the water-swollen polenta.

❹ Cook over low heat for about 40 minutes, stirring as often as you can. It will sputter and spit and, if it isn't stirred regularly, it will burn and stick to the base too. Add more water if needed. Polenta is done when it is a thick and creamy porridge consistency.

❺ Stir in a generous sprinkling of Parmesan cheese, a dash of nutmeg and butter as desired, then serve with the tomato-mushroom sauce ladled over it, and a final sprinkling of Parmesan.

*grains*

91

# Rich Risotto of Many Mushrooms

*A wide variety of mushrooms is what gives this risotto its charm. Instead of basil, try serving the risotto with a finishing of shaved truffles, or more prosaically, a little chive butter.*

SERVES 4

- 350–450 g/12–16 oz mixed fresh mushrooms, or common cultivated mushrooms combined with 50–75 g/2–3 oz rehydrated dried mushrooms, diced
- 65–75 g/2½–3 oz butter, olive oil or a combination
- 5–8 shallots, chopped
- 3–5 garlic cloves, chopped
- 200 g/7 oz Arborio rice
- 225 ml/8 fl oz dry white wine
- a grating of nutmeg
- 900 ml/1½ pints stock, or as needed
- 100 ml/4 fl oz single cream (optional)
- 4–6 Tbsp freshly grated Parmesan cheese, plus extra to serve
- a few basil leaves, thinly sliced, to garnish

**Preparation: 30-40 minutes**

**Cooking time : 40 minutes**

❶ Sauté the mushrooms in the butter and/or olive oil, until softened, then add the shallots and garlic. Cook a few minutes, then add the rice and cook, stirring, until it begins to turn golden.

❷ Stir in the wine and nutmeg, and cook over high heat, stirring, until the liquid evaporates. Then slowly add the stock, about 100 ml/4 fl oz at a time, stirring each time you add more liquid, and cooking until the liquid is absorbed.

❸ When the rice is *al dente*, stir in the cream, if using, and warm through.

❹ Stir in the Parmesan cheese, then serve immediately, garnished with basil. Offer extra Parmesan for people to help themselves.

# Risotto con Funghi e Salsiccia

**Red wine risotto with mushrooms and sausage**  *There is lots of room for creativity here, or for practicality—the risotto will be delicious whichever you choose.*

Serves 4

- 15 g/½ oz dried porcini, about 6 large slices
- 100 ml/4 fl oz water
- 50 g/2 oz butter
- 5 shallots, chopped
- 3 garlic cloves, chopped
- 1 Italian, anise- or fennel-flavoured sausage
- 100 g/4 oz common cultivated mushrooms, diced
- 300 g/11 oz Arborio rice
- 2 fresh ripe or canned tomatoes, finely diced
- 175 ml/6 fl oz red wine
- 1 pinch each rosemary, thyme and savory
- 750 ml/1¼ pints hot stock
- freshly grated Parmesan

**Preparation: 20-30 minutes**

**Cooking time : 40 minutes**

❶ Place the porcini and water in a saucepan. Bring to the boil, then simmer until tender. Leave to cool, then squeeze dry, saving the liquid. Roughly chop and set aside. Strain the liquid and set aside.

❷ Melt butter and sauté shallots and garlic until softened. Stir in the sausage and diced mushrooms. Cook until browned. Add the rice and cook for 5–10 minutes.

❸ Add the tomatoes, wine and herbs, then cook, stirring, until the moisture has evaporated. Stir in the mushroom liquid, then the stock, little by little, letting the rice absorb the liquid as you go (about 40 minutes).

❹ When the rice is *al dente*, stir in the mushrooms, warm through, then stir in a few spoonfuls of Parmesan cheese, adjusting for taste.

*grains*

# Couscous with Wild Mushrooms

*Though it's easy to think of couscous as the base for a hearty spicy vegetable or meat feast, it is equally delicious as a side dish. It pairs surprisingly well with wild mushrooms of all types, a fact not lost on North Africans when they are so lucky as to find a cache of mushrooms.*

SERVES 4

- 3–4 Tbsp mixed dried mushrooms
- scant 1 litre/1¾ pints vegetable stock or mushroom liquid if on hand
- 3–5 shallots or 1 onion, chopped
- 5 garlic cloves, chopped
- 40–50 g/1½–2 oz butter
- several pinches whole cumin seeds
- a small grating of nutmeg
- 350 g/12 oz instant couscous
- 100–175 g/4–6 oz Jarlsberg or Gruyère cheese, grated
- salt and ground black pepper, to taste

**Preparation: 25-30 minutes**
**Cooking time : 10-15 minutes**

❶ Combine the dried mushrooms with the stock or mushroom liquid, then bring to the boil. Reduce the heat and simmer 15 minutes, or until softened. Remove from the heat. When cool enough to handle, squeeze the mushrooms, saving all the liquid, then roughly chop and set aside.

❷ Strain the mushroom liquid, return it to the saucepan and cook over high heat until reduced by about one third.

❸ Meanwhile, lightly sauté the shallots or onion and garlic in two thirds of the butter until softened, then add the mushrooms and cook a few minutes more, until the mixture is golden brown. Season with the cumin and nutmeg.

❹ Pour the couscous into the boiling mushroom liquid and cook on low heat, stirring, for just a few minutes, or until the couscous absorbs the liquid. You do not want it to become mushy. Cover for a minute or two to plump up, then uncover and toss in the sautéed mushrooms, the remaining butter and the cheese. Season with salt and pepper, and serve immediately.

*grains*

Mushrooms of all types are superb cooked on the open fire of the grill or barbecue. The first time I tasted this method of cooking was predictably with porcini, grilled and drizzled with olive oil, as big as the plate and as satisfying as a steak. I've since then discovered that most mushrooms are terrific cooked on the fire, even plain ordinary cultivated ones. And if your mushrooms are too small to sit on top of the grid, skewer them, and then barbecue them.

# Barbecued Steak

## and Shiitake Mushrooms with Red Chilli-garlic Butter

*Cooking mushrooms on the barbecue creates the perfect accompaniment to big juicy steaks cooked outdoors. The earthy, smoky scent of the fire perfumes the fungi with its enticing aroma and flavour.*

SERVES 4

- 12 large shiitake mushrooms
- 4–5 Tbsp olive oil
- 8 garlic cloves, chopped
- 2 Tbsp lemon juice
- salt and ground black pepper, to taste
- 1 tsp chopped fresh thyme
- 1.25 kg/2½ lb fillet steak
- 3 Tbsp red wine

**For the Red Chilli-garlic Butter**

- 75 g/3 oz unsalted butter, softened
- 3–4 garlic cloves, chopped
- 1 tsp mild red chilli powder, or more to taste
- 1 tsp paprika
- ¼ tsp ground cumin, or to taste
- ½ tsp oregano or thyme leaves, crushed or chopped
- juice of ¼ lime or lemon
- salt, to taste

**Preparation: 40-45 minutes**

**Cooking time : 10-15 minutes**

❶ Marinate the mushrooms in half the olive oil, half the garlic, the lemon juice, some salt and half the thyme. Toss the steak in the remaining olive oil, garlic and thyme, and add the red wine. Leave both to marinate while you start the barbecue, for at least 30 minutes.

❷ Cook the steak and mushrooms on the barbecue or under a grill. If the shiitakes are too small to fit on the grid of the barbecue, and threaten to fall through, skewer them with soaked bamboo sticks or with metal skewers. Alternatively, use the grill.

❸ Combine the ingredients for red chilli-garlic butter and mix well.

❹ Barbecue the steak for about 8 minutes on each side for rare to medium rare, then remove from the barbecue, and place on a board. Keep warm while you barbecue the mushrooms. This rest will relax the fibres of the meat for a more tender dish.

❺ Cook the mushrooms for about 3 minutes on each side until juicy inside and nicely browned outside.

❻ Slice the steak about 2 cm/ ¾ inch against the grain. Serve each portion of steak with several mushrooms and a dollop of red chilli-garlic butter slathered on both steak and mushrooms, melting deliciously into a buttery sauce.

barbecuing & grilling

97

# Kebabs of Shiitake Mushrooms, Tofu and Onion

*This makes a good appetizer or a vegetarian main course served on a pile of Far Eastern rice pilaf. Sometimes I serve it with a spicy peanut sauce for dipping. It's delicious served at room temperature, too, so toss some on the barbecue, then enjoy them at room temperature as an appetizer the next day.*

SERVES 4

- 6–8 fresh shiitake mushrooms, quartered
- 350 g/12 oz tofu, cut into bite-size chunks
- 3–4 onions, cut into bite-size chunks
- 5 garlic cloves, chopped
- 3–5 Tbsp soy sauce
- 1 Tbsp lime or lemon juice
- several shakes of Tabasco sauce
- 2 Tbsp sesame oil
- ½ tsp ground cumin
- ¼ tsp ground coriander
- 1 Tbsp grated or finely chopped fresh root ginger
- several pinches Chinese five-spice powder
- 3 Tbsp vegetable oil
- bamboo skewers

**Preparation: 40-45 minutes**
**Cooking time : 5-10 minutes**

❶ Place the shiitakes, tofu and onions in a shallow, non-metallic pan and sprinkle with the remaining ingredients, turning everything so that it is all coated. Leave to marinate for at least 30 minutes and preferably overnight, turning several times.

❷ Soak the skewers in cold water for 30 minutes; this helps keep them from burning.

❸ Thread the shiitake, tofu and onion onto each skewer, then cook over medium heat on the barbecue. Serve hot or at room temperature.

# Barbecued Portobellos

SERVES 4

- 2 big portobellos or large flat mushrooms as a side dish, 4 as a main course
- 3–5 garlic cloves, chopped
- 2–3 Tbsp olive oil
- juice of ½ lemon or 1 Tbsp sherry or balsamic vinegar
- salt, ground black pepper and thyme, to taste

**Preparation: 25-40 minutes**
**Cooking time : 10 minutes**

*Be sure to marinate the portobellos for that extra dimension. Olive oil, lemon juice or balsamic or sherry vinegar, and lots of garlic or shallots, make the best marinade, boosted with fresh thyme, tarragon or parsley.*

❶ Sprinkle the mushrooms with the garlic, olive oil, lemon juice or vinegar and seasonings. Leave for 15–30 minutes.

❷ Cook on the barbecue, preferably one with a cover, ensuring the food is surrounded by hot, smoky heat. Turn once or twice, letting the mushrooms cook until lightly browned but juicy inside.

❸ Serve immediately, whole or sliced.

*barbecuing & grilling*

▲ Kebabs of Shiitake Mushrooms, Tofu and Onion

# Magret aux Porcini Grillé au Feu de Bois

**Barbecued duck breasts and porcini** *The southwest of France is known for its dishes with duck, and for its abundance of fungi, eaten in simple dishes such as the following one of grilled boneless duck breast and tasty foresty porcini. Begin the meal with a rustic French vegetable soup, drink a delicious Paulliac or Gaillac, and follow with a plate of delectable greens and a selection of glorious French cheeses.*

SERVES 4

- 4 half magrets (boned duck breasts)
- salt and ground black pepper, to taste
- 4 Tbsp red wine
- 5 garlic cloves, chopped
- 3 Tbsp olive oil
- 675 g/1½ lb porcini (or other large mushrooms)
- 2 Tbsp chopped fresh parsley

**Preparation: 15 minutes**

**Cooking time : 15 minutes**

❶ Score the skin of the magrets evenly, then place in a bowl and toss with salt, pepper, about half the wine, garlic and olive oil. Leave for at least an hour, while you prepare the barbecue.

❷ Toss the mushrooms with the remaining wine, garlic, olive oil and some salt and pepper. These do not need to marinate for long—a few minutes is fine.

❸ Cook the duck breasts and mushrooms over the fire, letting the fat cook off of the duck skin, then crisping up, but keeping the duck as rare as possible. Do this by cooking the skin side over a high heat, then the other side very quickly. It should only take about 5 minutes for the skin side, then a minute or two on the other.

❹ Cook the mushrooms a few minutes on each side, then serve the duck breasts cut thinly crossways (otherwise they tend to be tough) with the mushrooms, all sprinkled with parsley.

VARIATION:

Toulouse Sausages
with Porcini
Use meaty Toulouse sausages, small French sausages made from coarsely chopped pork flavoured with wine, garlic and seasonings, in place of the duck breasts.

As marvellous as mushrooms are with meats, fish, poultry and pasta, they are unsurpassed when eaten on their own or with whatever vegetable the season has to offer. Whether sautéed, gratinéed, simmered, chopped, stewed or grilled, the foresty flavour and scent of mushrooms adds its own special character and personality to your meal.

A bowl of stewed mushrooms – porcini, mousserons, trompettes de la mort, oyster, shiitakes, morels, enoki, even the simple cultivated ones – perfumed with a whiff of garlic and served with generous amounts of butter, their juices soaked up with hunks of crusty peasant bread; what could be a simpler, or more excellent feast?

*vegetable dishes*

# 'Lasagne' of Potatoes

## and Oyster and Shiitake Mushrooms

*Use any type of mushrooms you desire—the finished dish will taste of whichever you choose. If no fresh wild mushrooms are available, this is a fine dish to use ordinary white or brown mushrooms combined with dried mushrooms such as porcini, mixed mushrooms, trompettes de la mort.*

SERVES 4

- 4 large baking potatoes, peeled
- 350 g/12 oz fresh oyster and shiitake mushrooms
- 75 g/3 oz butter
- salt and black or cayenne pepper, to taste
- 1 Tbsp chopped fresh parsley or chervil, plus extra to serve
- 3 Tbsp chopped fresh tarragon, plus extra to serve
- 2 Tbsp flour
- 600 ml/1 pint milk
- several scrapings of nutmeg
- 5–7 Tbsp grated Parmesan cheese

**Preparation: 30 minutes**

**Cooking time : 1 hour**

❶ Parboil the potatoes in salted water until the potatoes' starch has just stabilized but they are still too crunchy to eat. This should take about 15 minutes at a gentle rolling simmer. Leave to cool in the water, then remove and slice thinly. They will be sticky at this point—don't worry.

❷ Preheat a 190°C/375°F/gas mark 5 oven. Sauté the mushrooms quickly and lightly in 50 g/2 oz of the butter until slightly browned and golden in places. Sprinkle with salt, pepper, parsley or chervil, and tarragon. Set aside.

❸ Make a béchamel sauce. Heat the remaining butter until melted then sprinkle in the flour. Heat until lightly golden, then remove from the heat. Meanwhile, heat the milk until bubbles form around the edge of the pan. Pour the milk into the flour mixture, return to the heat and stir until thickened.

Season with nutmeg, salt and black or cayenne pepper.

❹ Layer half the sliced potatoes in a buttered gratin or baking dish, cover with half the sautéed mushrooms, then with half the béchamel, then half the Parmesan cheese. Repeat, ending with the Parmesan cheese.

❺ Bake in the oven for 30–40 minutes, or until the potatoes are cooked through and the top of the 'lasagne' is light golden. Serve hot with additional chopped tarragon and a little parsley or chervil.

*vegetable dishes*

102

# Sauté of Chanterelles

## with a Crown of Crispy Potatoes

*This dish is very good, too, with a combination of mushrooms. Visit any countryside market in early autumn, and you will be faced with glorious abundance of fungi to choose from. They are not cheap, but they are thrilling, and well worth the expense.*

SERVES 4

- 3–4 large baking potatoes, peeled, soaked a few minutes in cold water, then dried and very thinly sliced
- olive oil or melted butter, for brushing
- 450 g/1 lb chanterelles or trompettes de la mort, cut into bite-size pieces
- 5 shallots, chopped
- 8 garlic cloves, chopped
- 3–5 Tbsp chopped fresh parsley
- 50 g/2 oz unsalted butter
- salt and ground black pepper, to taste
- a grating of nutmeg
- 100 ml/4 fl oz each red wine and vegetable or chicken stock

**Preparation: 20-30 minutes**
**Cooking time : 20-30 minutes**

❶ Preheat a 190°C/375°F/gas mark 5 oven. On a nonstick baking sheet, arrange four rounds, or concentric rings, of the potato slices, letting them stick together with their own juices. Brush with olive oil or melted butter, then bake in the oven until golden and crisply edged, about 25 minutes. They should stick together, but if they fall apart when you place them on top of the mushrooms, it doesn't really matter.

❷ While the potatoes bake, sauté the mushrooms with half the shallots, half the garlic and half the parsley in about 25 g/1 oz of the butter. Cook until lightly browned. Season with salt, pepper and nutmeg, then remove from the pan. Pour in the wine and stock, and boil down to a rich reduced essence of just a few tablespoons. Take care it does not overcook and turn bitter, however.

❸ Remove from the heat, swirl in the remaining butter, then return the mushrooms to the pan and toss with the sauce.

❹ Combine the remaining shallots, garlic and parsley in a small bowl. Serve each portion of mushrooms on a plate, topped with the potato 'crown', with the shallot-garlic-parsley mixture scattered over.

*vegetable dishes*

# Stir-fried Mushrooms

## with Courgettes and Onions

*Serve these flavourful vegetables with steamed jasmine rice, or on a bed of crispy noodles as chow mein.*

SERVES 4

- 3 onions, cut into bite-size chunks
- 2–3 Tbsp vegetable oil
- 5 garlic cloves, chopped
- 1–2 Tbsp roughly chopped fresh root ginger
- 2 courgettes, sliced diagonally
- 225–275 g/8–10 oz common cultivated or button mushrooms, quartered
- ½ stock cube, crumbled
- 75–100 ml/3–4 fl oz water
- 1½–2 tsp cornflour mixed with 2–3 Tbsp cold water
- 2 tsp soy sauce, or to taste
- 2 Tbsp chopped fresh coriander

**Preparation: 10-15 minutes**
**Cooking time : 10-15 minutes**

❶ Stir-fry the onions with a tiny amount of the oil over medium-high heat for just a moment, to lightly char rather than cook the onion. Add half the garlic and ginger, then the courgettes, and cook a few moments more, or until the courgettes are crisp yet tender. Remove from the pan.

❷ Add the remaining oil and stir-fry the mushrooms, adding the remaining garlic and ginger. Cook only for a few moments—they should remain crisp and fresh-looking, but be lightly browned in spots—then sprinkle in the stock cube and return the onions and courgettes to the pan.

❸ Gradually stir in the water and the cornflour paste (you may not need it all), cook a few moments, stir-frying, until the liquid thickens, then season with soy sauce. Serve immediately, with the coriander scattered over.

*vegetable dishes*

# Stir-fry of Black Mushrooms

## with Tofu and Green Vegetables

*This gentle, nourishing stir-fry combines protein-rich tofu with hearty black mushrooms and crisp, vibrant greens. It is one of my favourite dishes, one that I make whenever that call for comfort arises. Brown rice, with its earthy whole-grain flavour, makes an excellent accompaniment.*

SERVES 4

- 8–10 dried shiitake or Chinese black mushrooms
- 25 g/1 oz dried black tree cloud fungus
- 350 ml/12 fl oz hot, but not boiling, water
- 300–350 g/11–12 oz firm tofu
- 1 Tbsp cornflour, plus extra for dusting
- oil, for frying
- 2 carrots, thinly sliced diagonally
- 1 onion, thinly sliced lengthways
- 3–4 garlic cloves, chopped
- 2–3 Tbsp chopped fresh root ginger
- a large pinch or two of sugar
- 1 small bunch broccoli, cut into florets
- a handful of mangetout, topped and tailed
- 100 ml/4 fl oz hot chicken or vegetable stock
- 1 Tbsp soy sauce, or to taste
- 1 Tbsp sesame oil
- 1–2 Tbsp chopped fresh coriander

**Preparation: 45-50 minutes**

**Cooking time : 15-20 minutes**

❶ Rehydrate the shiitake or black mushrooms and tree cloud fungus by placing them in a saucepan with the hot water. Cover and leave to stand for 30 minutes. If they remain tough, bring the mushrooms, fungus and liquid to the boil, simmer a few minutes, then remove from the heat. Stand, covered, as before.

❷ Remove from the pan, strain the mushroom liquid, and reserve. If the tree cloud fungus is in large pieces, cut into bite-size ones. Leave the black mushrooms whole, or halve if they are very large. Set aside.

❸ Cut the tofu into bite-sized cubes, then dry well. Toss with cornflour to coat. Heat about 7.5 cm/3 inches of vegetable oil in a wok or deep frying pan. The oil is hot enough when a cube of bread sizzles and turns golden when dropped in. Carefully slip in the tofu cubes and cook until golden. They will spit, so beware. The cooking will take at least 5 minutes. Turn them occasionally and keep a close watch. They are at

their most delicious when golden and crisp on the outside and tender inside. When cooked, remove with a slotted spoon, and drain on absorbent kitchen paper.

❹ Pour off all the oil except for 1–2 tablespoons. Heat the wok or pan and stir-fry the carrots, onion, garlic and ginger. Sprinkle with sugar, cook a few minutes more and add the broccoli, reserved black mushrooms and tree cloud fungus, and a tablespoon or two of the mushroom liquid. Cover and cook for a moment, then remove the cover, let the liquid evaporate quickly, and add the mangetout.

❺ Mix the stock with an equal amount of the mushroom liquid, soy sauce and cornflour. Stir well, then stir this into the mixture and cook, stirring, until thickened.

❻ Turn onto a platter, drizzle with sesame oil, sprinkle with coriander. Serve immediately.

# Stir-fry of Broccoli

## *and Black Mushrooms in Hoisin Sauce with Cashews*

*Florets of crisp-tender, fresh green broccoli and soft, chewy earthy black mushrooms are cloaked in spicy-sweet hoisin sauce, and scattered with whole cashews. Baby corn or water chestnuts would also be good in the mélange.*

*Delicious as a side dish, as an accompaniment for something simple such as a roasted duck or steamed whole fish, along with a bowl of rice, or enjoy as a main course over wide rice noodles.*

SERVES 4

- 10–12 dried Chinese black mushrooms
- 1 onion, thinly sliced lengthways
- 3 garlic cloves, chopped
- 2 tsp chopped fresh root ginger
- 2 Tbsp vegetable oil, or as needed
- soy sauce, to taste
- 2 bunches broccoli, stalks peeled and cut into bite-size pieces, florets broken into bite-size pieces
- 1–2 tsp sugar, or more to taste
- 100 ml/4 fl oz stock
- 1–2 tsp cornflour mixed with 1 Tbsp water
- 1 Tbsp rice wine or sherry
- 4–5 Tbsp hoisin sauce
- a pinch each Chinese five-spice powder and white or cayenne pepper
- 50 g/2 oz toasted cashews, preferably dry roasted
- 1 Tbsp chopped fresh coriander
- ½ tsp sesame oil

**Preparation: 25-30 minutes**
**Cooking time : 10-15 minutes**

❶ Rehydrate the mushrooms by placing them in a saucepan with water to cover. Bring to the boil, then reduce the heat and simmer about 5 minutes. Stand for 10–15 minutes, then remove from the water and squeeze dry. Cut the stalks off, if they are tough, and set aside.

❷ Stir-fry the onion, garlic and ginger in half the oil, then add the mushrooms and cook a few moments. Sprinkle with soy sauce, cook a moment, then remove from the pan.

❸ Add the remaining oil, stir-fry the broccoli until it is crisp-tender, sprinkling with about ¼ teaspoon sugar as you stir-fry, then remove the broccoli from the pan.

❹ Add the stock and cornflour paste, stir until slightly thickened, then add the rice wine or sherry, hoisin sauce, five-spice powder, white or cayenne pepper and the remaining sugar. Cook a few minutes until slightly thickened.

❺ Return the mushrooms and broccoli to the pan, and toss in the cashews. Serve with the coriander and sesame oil.

*vegetable dishes*

# 'Cassoulet' of Porcini and White Beans

*Serve it with a salad of mesclun and a scattering of Roquefort. For a double mushroom meal, you might want to sauté a handful of oyster mushrooms and toss them, warm, onto the lightly dressed salad.*

SERVES 4

- 450 g/1 lb dried white beans, such as cannellini, soaked overnight
- 2 bay leaves
- 50 g/2 oz dried porcini or 25 g/1 oz dried porcini plus 225 g/8 oz fresh
- 1 onion, chopped
- 1 large baking potato, diced
- ½ carrot, diced
- 1 garlic bulb, cloves separated but left whole
- 4–6 Tbsp olive oil, or as needed
- salt and ground black pepper
- ¼ tsp dried herbes de Provence
- 350 ml/12 fl oz dry white wine
- 450 ml/¾ pint stock
- 150 g/5 oz fresh breadcrumbs
- 5 garlic cloves, chopped
- 3 Tbsp chopped fresh parsley

**Preparation: 30 minutes**

**Cooking time : 5 hours**

❶ Drain the soaked beans and place in a pan with the bay leaves and water to cover. Bring to the boil, reduce the heat and simmer over medium-low heat, covered, until tender, about 2 hours. Drain.

❷ Preheat a 170°C/325°F/gas mark 3 oven. Rehydrate the mushrooms in the water by bringing it to the boil, then reducing the heat and simmering a few minutes. Leave to plump up and cool. Remove from the water, chop roughly and set aside. Strain the liquid and set aside.

❸ Sauté the onion, potato, carrot and whole garlic cloves in about half the olive oil, until the onion is softened and the vegetables are golden. Season with salt, pepper and herbes de Provence. Pour in the wine, bring to the boil and cook over high heat, about 10 minutes.

❹ In a heavy casserole layer the beans, mushrooms, vegetables and wine, and stock. Bake in the oven for 1½ hours, about half the time covered, then with the cover removed. The beans should be creamy and tender by then.

❺ Mix the breadcrumbs with the chopped garlic and parsley. Spread about half this mixture over the beans, drizzle with half the remaining olive oil, then raise the oven temperature to 200°C/400°F/gas mark 6, and bake for about 15 minutes. Reduce the oven temperature to 190°C/375°F/gas mark 5 if you think there is a danger of burning the topping.

❻ With a spoon, break the crust and stir it into the cassoulet. Top with the remaining crumb mixture and drizzle over the rest of the olive oil, then return to the oven for another 15 minutes. Serve immediately.

*vegetable dishes*

# Potato and Mushroom Cakes

## on a Bed of Mixed Leaves

*Mashed potatoes are mixed with sautéed mushrooms, formed into cakes, then fried to a crisp. Serve on a bed of mixed leaves, with a wedge of lemon for squeezing, a mushroom sauce, or a little soured cream on the side, if desired.*

SERVES 4

- 1 Tbsp mixed dried mushrooms (optional)
- 350 g/12 oz fresh common cultivated or large flat mushrooms, chopped
- 2 onions, chopped
- 3 Tbsp olive oil
- 2 bay leaves
- 3 garlic cloves, chopped
- salt and ground black pepper, to taste
- 4 boiled potatoes, mashed
- 2 eggs, lightly beaten
- 2 Tbsp soured cream or cottage cheese
- 3 Tbsp breadcrumbs, plus extra for coating
- olive oil, for frying
- mixed leaves, to serve

**Preparation: 25 minutes**
**Cooking time : 45 minutes**

❶ If you are using dried mushrooms, rehydrate by placing in a saucepan with water to cover, then bring to the boil. Reduce the heat and simmer for 5–10 minutes. Remove from the heat. Take the mushrooms from the liquid, roughly chop, and set aside.

❷ Sauté all the mushrooms and the onions in the olive oil, with the bay leaves and garlic. When the onions are tender and the mushrooms browned, season with salt and pepper.

❸ In a large bowl, mix the mashed potato, egg, soured cream or cottage cheese and measured breadcrumbs. Add the mushroom mixture and combine well. Form patties with your hands, then coat each one in breadcrumbs.

❹ Chill for at least 30 minutes, then fry in a heavy-based frying pan in 1–2.5 cm/½–1 inch olive oil. Cook until crisp and browned. Keep the cakes warm as they are cooked, and serve on a bed of mixed leaves.

*vegetable diahes*

# Paprikash of Mushrooms

*Rich and russet hued from paprika, this is a simple sauté of mushrooms and peppers based on that Hungarian stew of meat or vegetables simmered with paprika and enriched with double or soured cream.*

*Serve with spaetzel, or noodles, or even Rumanian-style, over a mound of soft polenta.*

SERVES 4

- 2 onions, chopped
- 5 garlic cloves, chopped
- 40–65 g/1½–2½ oz butter, or less if desired
- 450 g/1 lb firm button, common cultivated white, or brown mushrooms, quartered
- ½ each fresh red and green pepper, diced
- 3–5 small fresh ripe tomatoes or about 175 g/6 oz canned, diced
- 1–2 Tbsp flour
- 2–3 tsp paprika, or more if desired
- ¼ tsp fresh thyme
- 100 ml/4 fl oz dry white wine
- 100 ml/4 fl oz stock
- 225 g/8 oz crème fraîche, or half ricotta cheese, half double or single cream
- salt and ground black pepper, to taste
- 3–5 spring onions, chopped, to garnish

**Preparation: 10-15 minutes**
**Cooking time : 15-30 minutes**

❶ Lightly sauté the onion and garlic in about half the butter until softened, then remove from the pan and set aside. Add the remaining butter to the pan. Sauté the mushrooms, then remove and set aside. In the same pan, cook the red and green peppers and tomatoes for a few moments, until softened a little. Sprinkle in the flour, cook a few minutes, then sprinkle in the paprika and thyme, and cook together for several minutes, taking care that the paprika does not burn.

❷ Return the onions and mushrooms to the pan, along with the wine and stock, and simmer for 15 minutes, until the vegetables are cooked. Stir the crème fraîche, or ricotta cheese mixture, season with salt and pepper, and warm through over gentle heat. Taste for seasoning and serve immediately, with the spring onions scattered over.

*vegetable dishes*

**109**

# Gratin aux Pommes de Terre

## et Trompettes de la Mort

**Gratin of potatoes and trompettes de la mort** *This exquisite gratin is a culinary souvenir from a winter stay in France's Jura. The mushrooms were pulled out of a huge jar, having been foraged for, then dried the previous autumn.*

SERVES 4

- 50 g/2 oz trompettes de la mort
- 225 ml/8 fl oz stock or water
- 8 baking potatoes (about 1.25 kg/2½ lb in total)
- 100 g/4 oz butter
- salt and ground black pepper, to taste
- 10 shallots, chopped or sliced
- 8–10 garlic cloves, chopped
- 350 ml/12 fl oz single cream
- 225 g/8 oz Parmesan, comte, fontina or Gruyère cheese, or a combination, grated, for sprinkling
- 1 Tbsp pink peppercorns
- 2 Tbsp chopped fresh parsley

**Preparation: 50 minutes**

**Cooking time : 40 minutes**

❶ Place the mushrooms in a saucepan with the stock or water and bring to the boil. Reduce the heat, simmer for 5–10 minutes, or until the mushrooms are tender, then remove from the heat. When mushrooms are cool enough to handle, remove from the saucepan, and set aside. Strain the mushroom liquid and set aside.

❷ Peel and thinly slice the potatoes, then place them in cold water to cover. Leave for about 30 minutes, then drain, and dry well. I like to use a clean tea towel and lay the potatoes in it, patting them all dry.

❸ Preheat a 190°C/375°F/gas mark 5 oven. Butter the base of a gratin dish and make a layer of the potatoes on the base. Sprinkle with salt, pepper, shallots and garlic, and add some little dots of butter, then make another layer of potatoes. Every so often, make a layer of the mushrooms. End with the potatoes, dotted with a tablespoon or so of the butter.

❹ Pour the reserved mushroom liquid over the potatoes, then pour the cream over and finally sprinkle with the cheese. Bake in the oven for about an hour, or until the top is crusty and browned and the potatoes are meltingly tender.

❺ Serve sprinkled with pink peppercorns and parsley.

*vegetable diabes*

# Roasted Oyster Mushrooms

## *with Tender Whole Garlic Cloves*

*Blanching whole unpeeled garlic cloves makes them tender and sweet. Any kind of oyster mushrooms are delicious, and a selection is quite fun, as you can discover the different qualities of each type in one dish. Or you might choose a selection of different mushrooms altogether. The mushrooms and poached garlic can be sautéed in a large heavy-based frying pan, in several batches, if needed, so as not to crowd the mushrooms.*

SERVES 4

- 2 garlic bulbs, cloves separated but unpeeled
- 450 ml/¾ pint vegetable or chicken stock
- 450 g/1 lb oyster mushrooms, whole but broken into clumps
- 75 g/3 oz butter or olive oil, or as desired
- 2 garlic cloves, chopped
- several sprigs fresh thyme
- 1 Tbsp chopped fresh parsley or snipped fresh chives

**Preparation: 10-15 minutes**

**Cooking time : 50 minutes**

❶ Preheat a 180°C/350°F/gas mark 4 oven. Simmer the whole garlic cloves in the stock until almost tender and the liquid has reduced by about half, about 10 minutes.

❷ Place the mushrooms in a roasting tin. Surround with the garlic cloves and drizzle with the stock. Stud the top of the mushrooms and the garlic cloves with the butter or drizzle with the olive oil, sprinkle with chopped garlic and thyme, then roast for 20–30 minutes. If they are not done, raise the oven temperature to 190–200°C/375°–400°F/gas mark 5–6, and roast for 5–10 minutes.

❸ Serve sprinkled with parsley or chives.

TIP:

Don't throw out the garlic poaching liquid. It is great for making soups or for adding to vegetable or meat stocks.

# Manitaria Afelia

**Mushrooms afelia-style** *Afelia-style is a particular Cypriot style of cooking involving stewing foods in red wine with coriander seeds. Serve as part of the parade of little dishes that makes up a meze dinner, or as a hot appetizer, accompanied by crusty bread.*

SERVES 4 AS AN APPETIZER, SIDE DISH OR SEPARATE VEGETABLE COURSE

- 1–2 Tbsp each olive oil and butter
- 1 onion, chopped
- 4 garlic cloves, roughly chopped
- 450 g/1 lb fairly small button mushrooms, quartered
- 225 ml/8 fl oz red wine
- 225 ml/8 fl oz beef or vegetable stock
- 1 Tbsp coarsely crushed coriander seeds
- a pinch of ground cumin
- salt and ground black pepper, to taste
- a squeeze of lemon juice

**Preparation: 10 minutes**

**Cooking time : 20 minutes**

❶ Melt the olive oil and butter together over low heat in a large, heavy-based sauté or frying pan, add the onion and gently sauté until softened.

❷ Add the garlic and mushrooms, and sauté over medium-high heat

until the mushrooms are lightly browned—you may need to do this in several batches so that they brown and do not become watery. As they are cooked, remove the mushrooms, with the onion, to a plate.

❸ Pour the wine and stock into the pan, with the coriander seeds and cumin. Bring to the boil and cook over high heat until reduced to about 100–150 ml/4–5 fl oz.

❹ Return the mushrooms and onion (and any juices that have accumulated) to the pan. Cook over high heat about 5 minutes, or until the mushrooms are tender. Season with salt, pepper and a squeeze of lemon juice. Serve immediately.

*vegetable dishes*

# Garlicky Mashed Potatoes

## with Wild Mushrooms

*Rich and wintery, this makes a comforting dish to enjoy on a chilly night either alongside a meaty main course, or as its own course, served in a bowl and eaten with a spoon.*

SERVES 4

- 225 g/8 oz fresh mushrooms or 15 g/½ oz mixed dried mushrooms, or all porcini
- 100 g/4 fl oz water, if using dried mushrooms
- 4 baking potatoes, cut into chunks
- 10 garlic cloves, 5 whole, 5 chopped
- 4 Tbsp olive oil
- 2 Tbsp mushroom jus (see page 127) or brandy, if using fresh mushrooms
- 100 ml/4 fl oz single cream
- salt and ground black pepper, to taste
- 3–5 Tbsp snipped fresh chives

**Preparation: 20 minutes**
**Cooking time : 30 minutes**

❶ If using fresh mushrooms, chop them roughly. If using dried mushrooms, rehydrate by placing in a saucepan with the water, bringing to the boil, then reducing the heat, and simmering for about 5 minutes. Leave the mushrooms to cool for at least 15 minutes, then remove from the water. Squeeze dry, roughly chop and set aside. Strain the mushroom liquid, then bring to the boil, and reduce to 2 tablespoons.

❷ Meanwhile, cook the potatoes together with the whole garlic cloves in lightly salted water to cover. When tender, drain and mash.

❸ Heat the olive oil in a frying pan and toss in the chopped garlic and the mushrooms. Warm through, then add the 2 tablespoons mushroom jus, brandy, or reduced mushroom liquid, and cook down until evaporated.

❹ Mix this into the mashed potatoes, along with the cream, salt and pepper, and chives. Taste for seasoning, and serve with the addition of a nugget of butter to melt on top, if you like.

# Spanish Roasted Mushrooms

*This simple Mediterranean dish of roasted mushrooms is sprinkled with fino sherry, garlic and butter, with a scattering of almonds, which toast while the mushrooms cook.*

SERVES 4

- 450 g/1 lb large flat mushrooms
- 1 Tbsp fino sherry
- 5 garlic cloves, chopped
- 40 g/1½ oz butter
- 1 Tbsp chopped fresh parsley
- salt and ground black pepper, to taste
- 3–4 Tbsp flaked almonds

**Preparation: 10 minutes**

**Cooking time : 20 minutes**

❶ Preheat a 200°C/400°F/gas mark 6 oven. Arrange the mushrooms on a large baking sheet and sprinkle the sherry, then the garlic, over the top. Dot with the butter, sprinkle with parsley, salt, pepper and almonds.

❷ Bake in the oven until the mushrooms sizzle and the nuts are toasted, about 20 minutes. Serve immediately.

*vegetable diabes*

114

# Haricots aux Champignons et Aubergine

**Tender white beans with mixed mushrooms, wine, tomatoes and aubergine** *This stewy mélange, with its earthy scent of mushrooms, hearty beans and meaty aubergine, is decidedly appetizing. Serve it in a rustic ceramic casserole, accompanied by crusty bread for dipping into, and follow with a countryside salad of chicory and herbs, and perhaps a slab or two of Roquefort.*

SERVES 4

- 225 g/8 oz dried white beans, soaked overnight
- 2 bay leaves
- 3–4 Tbsp mixed dried mushrooms, such as forest mix containing porcini, trompettes de la mort and morels or mousserons
- 1 medium-large onion, chopped
- 5 garlic cloves, roughly chopped
- 75–100 ml/3–4 fl oz extra virgin olive oil, plus extra if needed and to finish
- 350–400 g/12–14 oz fresh ripe tomatoes or canned with their juice, diced
- 350 ml/12 fl oz red wine
- several sprigs of fresh thyme
- salt and ground black pepper, to taste
- a pinch of sugar, or to taste
- 1 smallish aubergine, cut into bite-size pieces
- chopped fresh parsley

**Preparation: 20-25 minutes**

**Cooking time : 1½ hours**

❶ Place the soaked beans and bay leaves in a saucepan, with fresh water to cover. Bring to the boil, then reduce the heat, and cook over medium-low heat until the beans are ready, about 1 hour, depending on the bean you use. (Check the instructions on the packet.)

❷ A half hour before the beans will be cooked through, add the dried mushrooms. Cook until the beans are tender and the mushrooms rehydrated. Spoon the beans and mushrooms from the pot and place in a bowl. Strain the liquid, and set aside.

❸ Meanwhile, sauté the onion and half the garlic in a few tablespoons of the olive oil and, when softened, add the tomatoes. Cook over medium-high heat until saucelike, then add the wine and thyme. Cook over medium-high heat until the wine has nearly evaporated. Adjust seasoning, and add sugar to taste. Then set aside.

❹ Brown the aubergine in the remaining olive oil, adding extra if needed. When tender but browned, remove from the pan.

❺ In a frying pan, combine the beans and mushrooms with the tomato mixture, aubergine and the beans and strained mushroom liquid. Cook over high heat, stirring occasionally but gently so as not to break up the beans, until the liquid is reduced to a reasonable amount. Season with salt, and stir in a little extra olive oil to taste. Serve garnished with chopped fresh parsley.

TIP:

Choose any white bean you like. Although butter beans taste lovely, they tend to go mushy, and fall apart. I go for Greek fasoulia gigantes, French lingots or Italian cannellini.

*vegetable dishes*

Whether eaten as an appetizer, cut into small pieces as antipasti, or enjoyed as a mid-afternoon snack or supper, pizza, savoury tarts and zesty mixtures—either spooned onto bread or rolled into tortillas—are the perfect vehicle for the versatile mushroom.

## pizzas & bread dishes

Wild and tamed mushrooms are all delicious, either on their own or in conjunction with each other. And the dishes that follow range from unashamedly luxurious—such as Pizza ai Porcini e Tartuffe (see page 119), which is packed with porcini and truffles—to down to earth. Enjoy!

# Crostini alla Funghi

**Marsala-scented mushrooms on crisp toasts with melted cheese**

*This makes a marvellous spuntino, or little afternoon snack, with a glass of wine to wash it down.*

Serves 4

- 50 g/2 oz butter
- 1 onion, finely chopped
- 3–4 garlic cloves, chopped
- 350 g/12 oz mixed fresh mushrooms, such as porcini, ordinary white or black mushrooms, oyster mushrooms, trompettes de mort and shiitakes, dried or roughly chopped
- 2–3 Tbsp Marsala
- several gratings of nutmeg
- 3 Tbsp double cream
- 5 Tbsp fromage frais or ricotta cheese
- 3–5 Tbsp freshly grated Parmesan cheese
- salt and ground black pepper, to taste
- 8–12 slices of baguette or close-crumbed bread, cut into fingers

**Preparation: 10-15 minutes**
**Cooking time : 20-25 minutes**

❶ Melt the butter, then sauté the onion, garlic and mushrooms together until lightly browned. Pour in the Marsala and evaporate over high heat.

❷ Remove from the heat and add the nutmeg, cream, fromage frais or ricotta cheese and Parmesan. Season with salt and pepper.

❸ Lightly toast both sides of the bread, then spread one side with the cheese mixture. Grill until lightly browned on top, then serve hot.

# Basic Pizza Dough

*The pizza is a wonderfully versatile dish, allowing for great creativity in devising different toppings.*

*Use this dough recipe for your pizza and calzone bases. The water should be at body temperature; test it against the back of your wrist.*

MAKES 1 30-CM/12-INCH ROUND PIZZA

- 350 g/12 oz plain flour
- ½ tsp salt
- 1 envelope dried yeast
- a pinch of sugar
- about 225 ml/8 fl oz warm water
- 5 Tbsp olive oil

**Rising time : 1-1½ hours at room temperature**

**Cooking time : 15-25 minutes**

❶ Preheat a 220°C/425°F/gas mark 7 oven. Sift the flour and stir in the salt, yeast and sugar. Make a well in the centre.

❷ Reserve 3–4 tablespoons of the water, mix the rest with the oil, then pour it into the well. Using your hands, gradually mix the flour into the liquid, a little at a time, from the sides of the bowl, until the mixture combines to form a soft dough. If it seems too dry, add a little more water.

❸ Turn the dough out onto a lightly floured board and knead for about 10 minutes, or until smooth, elastic and with a satiny sheen. When you poke your finger in, the dough should spring back out. If it remains too sticky, knead in a little more flour.

❹ Place the dough in an oiled bowl, cover with a clean tea towel, plastic bag or cling film, and leave in a warm place until doubled in size. An airing cupboard or warm kitchen will make for quicker

rising—about 1–1½ hours. (If you would like to make the dough ahead of time, let it rise a day or two in the refrigerator, taking care that it is loosely wrapped to allow for expansion.)

❺ Knock back the dough, then leave to rise again. This time will be a lot quicker. (Again, you can do this in the refrigerator to suit your timing.)

❻ When ready to make your pizza, roll out the dough to fit a 30-cm/12-inch, round, lightly oiled pizza pan, or place on a lightly oiled baking sheet, pressing the dough to form a slightly raised edge. Add your chosen topping.

❼ Bake in the oven for about 15–20 minutes, or until golden brown.

# Pizza ai Porcini e Tartuffe

**Pizza with porcini and truffles** *Mushrooms and delicate mozzarella cheese make a lovely combination. Using them to top a pizza, combined with a heady dose of truffle, is a speciality of Norcia, the Umbrian town as famous in Italy for its truffles as the Périgord is in France.*

SERVES 4
- 1 quantity Basic Pizza Dough (see opposite)
- 75 g/3 oz dried porcini
- 1 large black flat mushroom or 225 g/8 oz fresh mushrooms, such as trompettes de mort or porcini
- 3 Tbsp olive oil
- salt and ground black pepper, to taste
- 3 garlic cloves, chopped
- 350 g/12 oz mozzarella cheese, coarsely grated
- 25 g/1 oz truffle/porcini or truffle condiment
- 3–4 Tbsp freshly grated Parmesan or pecorino cheese
- a few drops of truffle oil, to serve (optional)

**Preparation (excluding dough time) : 15 minutes**
**Cooking time : 25 minutes**

❶ Roll out the dough and use to line an oiled pizza pan or four individual tins. Set aside.

❷ Rehydrate the dried mushrooms by placing them in a pan with water to cover and simmering until tender, about 10 minutes. Remove from the heat and, when cool enough to handle, squeeze dry.

❸ Preheat a 200°C/400°F/gas mark 6 oven. Lightly sauté the rehydrated and fresh mushrooms in the olive oil, until the fresh mushrooms are wilted and soft. Add salt, pepper and the garlic. Leave to cool.

❹ Spread half the cheese over the pizza base(s). Top with the mushrooms, add dollops of the truffle/porcini or truffle condiment, another layer of mozzarella cheese and a sprinkling of Parmesan or pecorino.

❺ Bake in the oven for 20–25 minutes, or until the topping is melted and sizzling, and the dough bubbly and cooked through. Serve immediately, with a few drops of truffle oil, if desired.

# Pizza ai Funghi e Pomadori

**Tomato and mushroom pizza** *Tomatoes and mushrooms have a natural affinity. This pizza topping creates a wonderfully deep and rich flavour, which is lifted by the inclusion of fresh oregano.*

SERVES 4

- 1 quantity Basic Pizza Dough (see page 118)
- 4 Tbsp tomato purée (optional)
- 100 ml/4 fl oz passata
- 2–3 fresh ripe or canned tomatoes, diced
- 2 garlic cloves, chopped
- 1 tsp fresh oregano, crumbled
- 225 g/8 oz common cultivated mushrooms, white or brown, thinly sliced
- 350 g/12 oz mozzarella cheese, or half mozzarella, half fontina, grated
- 2 Tbsp olive oil
- freshly grated Parmesan cheese, to taste

**Preparation: 10 minutes**

**Cooking time : 20 minutes**

❶ Preheat a 200°C/400°F/gas mark 6 oven. Roll out the dough and use to line an oiled pizza pan. Spread the dough with the tomato purée, if using, then drizzle with the passata.

❷ Scatter the tomatoes, garlic, oregano, mushrooms and mozzarella cheese, or mozzarella and fontina cheeses, over the top. Drizzle with the olive oil and sprinkle with as much Parmesan cheese as you like.

❸ Bake in the oven for 15–20 minutes, or until the cheeses have melted and turned golden in spots, and the crust is golden and its edges have risen.

*pizzas and bread dishes*

120

# Bruschetta di Funghi Misti

*con Pane Rosemarino e Due Formaggio*

**Sautéed mixed mushrooms with rosemary focaccio, goat's cheese and mozzarella cheese** *Quick and easy to prepare, these bruschetta make a flavourful lunchtime treat, especially when washed down with a glass of robust red wine.*

SERVES 4
- 450 g/1 lb mixed fresh exotic mushrooms, roughly chopped
- 4 garlic cloves, chopped
- 4–6 Tbsp olive oil
- salt and ground black pepper, to taste
- chopped fresh rosemary, to taste
- 4 slices focaccio
- 1 garlic clove, halved
- 100 g/4 oz goat's cheese, thinly sliced
- 100 g/4 oz mozzarella cheese, thinly sliced
- 3 Tbsp chopped fresh parsley

**Preparation: 20 minutes**
**Cooking time : 20 minutes**

❶ Lightly sauté the mushrooms and garlic in a heavy-based frying pan in the olive oil, until the mushrooms are golden. Season, add rosemary, and set aside.

❷ Toast one side of the focaccio slices, then turn them over and rub the tops with the halved garlic clove. Add layers of goat's cheese and mozzarella to each one.

❸ Grill the bruschetta until the cheeses melt. Meanwhile heat the mushrooms, tossing, until they are quite hot. Serve the cheese-topped toasts immediately, with the mushroom mixture spooned over, and sprinkled with chopped parsley.

# Wild Mushroom Quesadillas

*Quesadillas are no more than melted cheese sandwiches, Mexican-style, made on a flat corn or flour tortilla instead of on bread. Anything can be added to them: savoury stewed and chillied meats are a traditional treat, while vegetarian fillings such as barbecued or grilled vegetables or sautéed wild mushrooms add an innovative, contemporary flair.*

SERVES 4

- 1 onion, chopped
- 5 garlic cloves, chopped
- 3–4 Tbsp olive oil
- 225 g/8 oz mixed fresh mushrooms, chopped
- a pinch of ground cumin
- salt and ground black pepper, to taste
- 1–2 Tbsp finely chopped fresh coriander
- 8 smallish fresh corn tortillas
- 350 g/12 oz cheese, such as fontina, mozzarella, asiago, or any mild white cheese that melts well, grated
- bottled hot sauce, to serve

**Preparation: 10-15 minutes**
**Cooking time : 15-20 minutes**

❶ Sauté the onion and garlic in the olive oil until softened, then add the mushrooms and cook, turning, until lightly browned and tender. This will depend on the mushrooms you choose. Season with cumin, salt and pepper, sprinkle with the coriander, then set aside and keep warm.

❷ To make the quesadillas, warm the tortillas either in a heavy-based, lightly greased frying pan or stack, unwrapped on a plate, and microwave at full power for about 60 seconds. When they are warm, take each one and sprinkle with cheese. Working one at a time, keep them warm and supple by covering the stack of tortillas not yet being used with a damp absorbent kitchen paper. Fold over and heat through again, one at a time, either in the microwave or the frying pan. When the cheese

has melted, open the tortilla and stuff some of the mushrooms inside. Serve immediately, with bottled hot sauce. (If you like, place each one as it is made on a baking sheet, cover lightly, and keep warm in a low oven until

TIP:

Select some flavourful and some milder-tasting mushrooms, such as oysters, trompettes de la mort and common cultivated.

122

# Croûtes aux Morilles et Champignons Varis

**Morel and other mushrooms in cheese fondue gratinéed on toast**

*These dreamy mushroom and cheese toasts are so moreish, you may want to make double quantities. The amounts given here would serve double.*

SERVES 8

- 25 g/1 oz dried morel mushrooms
- 225 ml/8 fl oz hot, but not boiling, water
- 175–225 g/6–8 oz mixed fresh mushrooms, such as ordinary button mushrooms, oysters, morels, trompette de la mort, and porcini
- 100 ml/4 fl oz dry white wine
- 100 ml/4 fl oz vegetable or chicken stock
- 350 g/12 oz white cheese, such as comte, Gruyère, mild white Cheddar or fontina, grated
- 1 garlic clove, finely chopped
- a few gratings fresh nutmeg
- 60–75 ml/2–3 fl oz double cream or crème fraîche
- salt and ground black pepper, to taste
- 8 slices pain levain or other flavourful country bread
- 3–4 Tbsp snipped fresh chives

**Preparation: 30 minutes**

**Cooking time : 15 minutes**

❶ Place the dried morels in a bowl and pour over the hot water. Leave to stand for at least 30 minutes. When cool enough to handle, remove from the liquid and squeeze dry, saving the liquid. Strain the mushroom liquid and set aside.

❷ Slice the dried and fresh mushrooms, and combine in a saucepan with the mushroom liquid, wine and stock. Bring to the boil, then reduce the heat and simmer for 5–8 minutes, or until the mushrooms are just tender.

❸ Stir in the cheese, garlic, nutmeg and cream or crème fraîche, cooking over medium-low heat until the cheese melts and the texture is like a fondue. Season with salt and black pepper.

❹ Toast the bread lightly on both sides, then arrange on a baking sheet. Spoon the mushroom mixture over the top. Grill until the tops sizzle slightly, then serve immediately, with the chives scattered over.

*pizzas and bread dishes*

**123**

# Panino alla Funghi

**Sautéed mushrooms and fresh mozzarella cheese roll sandwich**

*Among the enticing, freshly made sandwiches, offered by Italian cappuccino bars, are ones filled with meat, fish, salads and vegetables. I especially like sandwich rolls of sautéed mushrooms and mozzarella cheese, with the juices all being soaked up deliciously into the absorbent bread.*

SERVES 4

- 225–350 g/8–12 oz common cultivated mushrooms, sliced
- 2 Tbsp olive oil, plus extra for drizzling
- 2 garlic cloves, chopped
- salt, to taste
- a large pinch of thyme
- 4 crusty French rolls, split into halves
- 200 g/7 oz mozzarella cheese (including packing water), sliced

**Preparation: 10 minutes**

**Cooking time : 5 minutes**

❶ Lightly sauté the mushrooms in the olive oil with the garlic until golden brown. Season with salt and thyme, then leave to cool.

❷ Drizzle a little extra olive oil over the cut sides of the rolls then layer first the mozzarella cheese, then the mushroom mixture. Close up and enjoy.

*pizzas and bread dishes*

This whole book is awash in sauces: delicious, mushroomy, interesting sauces. Throughout, you will find plenty of cream, reductions of wine, essences of herbs and gutsy mixtures of tomato and sausage, all coating any of the myriad types of earthy mushrooms and fungi.

Following are a handful of useful sauces for your repertoire that can go nearly anywhere.

# Wild Mushroom and Chipotle Salsa

*The smoky scent of chipotles deliciously sets off the hearty flavour of wild mushrooms. Since the mushrooms are going to be overpowered to a degree, do not use anything too subtle or too expensive. I like an assortment of shiitakes, with a few mousserons, trompettes de la mort, slices of porcini, and so forth.*

*The salsa is delicious with tacos, tostadas and tortillas, or anything from the barbecue, such as barbecued corn on the cob or duck.*

- 25 g/1 oz dried mushrooms or 175–225 g/6–8 oz fresh, including oysters, trompettes de la mort and other fleshy mushrooms
- ½ onion or 3 shallots, chopped
- 3 garlic cloves, sliced
- 2–3 Tbsp olive oil
- 1–2 pinches whole cumin seeds
- ¼–½ tsp mild chilli powder, such as ancho
- 4 fresh ripe tomatoes or canned (plus 4–5 Tbsp juice), diced
- ½ or more chipotle chilli in adobo, chopped or mashed, or a few shakes of bottled chipotle
- juice of ½ lemon or lime
- 2 Tbsp chopped fresh coriander
- salt, to taste

**Preparation: 10-15 minutes**
**Cooking time : 10-20 minutes**

❶ Rehydrate the dried mushrooms, if using, by either soaking or simmering in hot water until tender. When cool enough to handle, squeeze dry, then chop roughly. You should have about 8 heaped tablespoons of mushrooms. If using fresh mushrooms, clean and chop roughly.

❷ Lightly sauté the onion or shallots and garlic in the olive oil, then sprinkle in the cumin seeds. Add the mushrooms, cook for a few moments, then sprinkle with the chilli powder. Add the tomatoes and cook until reduced to a salsa-like mixture. Then add the chipotle, lemon or lime juice and coriander. Add salt to taste and serve as desired.

VARIATION:
Add the corn kernels of two corn on the cobs, slightly scorched in a lightly oiled heavy-based frying pan or left over from a meal cooked on the barbecue.

# Duxelles

*This is the classic French paste of cooked-down mushrooms, sautéed very, very slowly, with additions of brandy, salt, pepper and butter, until the mixture cooks down to its essence.*

*Use it as a spread for crostini or thin toasty canapés, or as a filling for chicken breasts, or to enrich sauces for pastas or soups. It is a good way of using up stalks and odd pieces of mushroom.*

*Duxelles can be frozen for up to about 2 months.*

- 8 shallots, chopped
- 50 g/2 oz butter, preferably unsalted
- 1 kg/2¼ lb fresh mushrooms, either mixed wild, a combination of common cultivated and wild, or all one type, roughly chopped
- salt, ground black pepper and grated nutmeg, to taste

**Preparation: 10-15 minutes**
**Cooking time : 20-30 minutes**

❶ Sauté the shallots in the butter for a minute or two, then add the mushrooms. Cook very slowly and evenly until the liquid that seeps out of the mushrooms is evaporated. Season with salt, pepper and nutmeg, and leave to cool.

❷ For a smooth consistency, chop the mushrooms finely by hand or whiz in a blender or food processor.

❸ If you are going to freeze, place the mixture in ice-cube trays, freeze, then pop into plastic bags. Use as desired.

# Mushroom Jus

*This makes a small amount of intensely flavoured mushroom liquid, delicious added to mustard, cream sauces, mashed potatoes, sautéed mushrooms and gratinéed dumplings, or drizzled onto a plate as a tasty decoration, for example around a risotto.*

- 450 ml/¾ pint strained mushroom liquid
- ¼ stock cube

**Preparation: 5 minutes**
**Cooking time : 15-30 minutes**

❶ Place the mushroom liquid in a saucepan and bring to the boil. Cook over high heat until reduced by about half, then add the ¼ stock cube. Continue to boil until reduced to about 5 tablespoons.

*sauces & salsas*

127

# Index